Proud
Spirit

Proud
Spirit

Lessons, Insights & Healing from
"The Voice of the Spirit World"
ROSEMARY ALTEA

EAGLE BROOK
WILLIAM MORROW AND COMPANY, INC.
New York

Published by Eagle Brook
An Imprint of William Morrow and Company Inc.
1350 Avenue of the Americas, New York, N.Y. 10019

Library of Congress Cataloging-in-Publication Data

Altea, Rosemary.
    Proud spirit : lessons, insights & healing from "the voice of the spirit world" / Rosemary Altea.
      p.   cm.
    ISBN 0-688-16067-0
    1. Future life.   2. Spiritualism.   3. Spiritual healing.   4. Grey Eagle (Spirit)   I. Title.
    BF1311.F8A56   1997
    133.9—dc21   96-40333
                                                                CIP

Printed in the United States of America

First Paperback Edition 1998

9   10

BOOK DESIGN BY GIORGETTA BELL MCREE

www.williammorrow.com

For the spirit world, whose voice is finally heard.

For my child, Samantha, without whose love and light I could not exist.

For Jim, who has given us
a small glimpse of his private heart,
and allowed us to share his own
personal struggle to become a Proud Spirit.
My love and gratitude.

ACKNOWLEDGMENTS

First, my thanks to Sally, who is a constant source of pleasure to me. Always smiling, caring, and sensitive in her work, she runs my office in England with smoothness and efficiency. Please don't leave me, Sal.

To my good friend and editor, Joann Davis, without whom this book would be so much less than it is. To my friend Joni Evans, who from the beginning of my writing career has been a constant source of support. I value her friendship. To say more of these two women who have played such a large part in my life over the last three years, to talk of their journey with me, I will say only that they have an equal place in my heart and my eternal gratitude.

To my many friends, my team of healers.

I would especially like to thank all those who read my first book, *The Eagle and the Rose*, and wrote to me to express their enjoyment of my work, and their pleasure in getting to know me a little.

There are so many, many people who in one way or another have given so much, and I would like to thank them all.

Acknowledgments

But there is one to whom I must give special mention to. One who knows the true meaning of the word friendship. One who has been unfailing in her loyalty, her support, her love, and her caring of me, for no other reason than that I call her friend, and that she calls me friend. She is my greatest ally, and aside from Grey Eagle, she is my closest and dearest friend. I love you, Joan, and from deep within my heart, I thank you.

Grey Eagle and I join together in thanking you all.

CONTENTS

CONTENTS

Question: Grey Eagle, why are we here in the first place?

Answer: Learning. Mortal beings, placed on earth, begin a learning process. Growth, self-growth ... is an intimate thing. It is between you and your soul. Your soul is wise beyond all recognition.

The heart of the soul throbs. The heart of the soul is light.

"Like a bulb, the soul is planted. In good soil, its roots go deep into the earth. Its only needs, light and love. And given those, it surely will flower."

Proud Spirit

PRELUDE

It was morning, 7:30 a.m., and although she wasn't sleeping, she was snuggled down in bed, enjoying those last lazy moments before getting up. The night before had been fun. Kay and Claire had come over for dinner, and as they had stayed late, both had decided to sleep over. Claire, a nurse, on early duty at the hospital, had to be up and out by 5:30 a.m. Kay had already gone, having popped her head around the bedroom door to say a hasty goodbye before chasing off home, late for college.

Lazily, she stretched, yawned, and peered over the quilt at the clock on the bedside table, now registering 7:45 a.m. "Just ten more minutes and I'll get up," she thought, wanting to enjoy every last second before she began her busy day.

It was at that moment that she heard the footsteps. Someone was walking across the landing toward the bathroom, which was right next to her bedroom.

"Oh no," she thought. "Poor Claire must have overslept." At this, the bedroom door opened and Claire came in.

She didn't lift her head from the pillow but watched with half-closed eyes as Claire walked past her around the bed. Then, a strange thing—she felt the bedcovers being lifted back, felt the bed sink down as Claire climbed in, and as she turned over to ask her friend what on earth she thought she was doing, felt Claire's leg push hard against her own. . . . and as she sat, and turned, her mouth, uttering the words. . . . "What do you think . . . ?" She froze, totally disbelieving what she saw . . . for there was no one there.

Two weeks went by. Again, it was early morning, around 7:00 a.m. She came out of sleep, lying on her side. Half turning, she stretched, and moved her leg to the far side of the bed. Again she froze. Incredulous, panic mounting, she couldn't move. An arm, a man's arm, reached across her, pulled her close to him. Too scared to scream, to move even, she lay quite still, her heart thudding in her chest. She could hear his breathing now, slow and easy. His grip on her tightening just a fraction, he pulled her closer still. Oddly her panic subsided. His movement had caused her to be strangely comforted. Whoever he was, he did not seem to want to harm her. A million thoughts raced through her head. A thief . . . burglar . . . rapist . . . who?

His arm was strong and unbending. She could feel the warmth from his body, his knees tucked into hers, his breathing regular, almost as if he were asleep. Scared, but now less and less panicked, slowly she lifted her head and peered over her shoulder. . . . and she could feel him, and she could hear him, but she could not see him. . . . for there was no one there.

Was it a visitor from the spirit world, or was it someone from the earth plane astral-traveling? She ponders this question once again, even as she writes. And once again, there is no answer.

She pauses, her pen hovers over the page. . . . she reflects back, remembering many incidents like these throughout her life. Which ones will she write about? This is her life. . . .

INTRODUCTION

There are many things I have to tell you, much information I want to impart, about the spirit world and the people of the spirit world. In this book I must tell you more of their story, and how we who live on this earth, how our actions and our thoughts, create reactions in the world of spirit. I would also like to tell you about what happens when we die, how through our lives we have lessons and can gain insight. And as healing is a big part of my life, I will share many stories with you on this subject as well.

If you come with me on this journey I will present more stories in a casebook section similar to the one so many of you enjoyed in my first book, *The Eagle and the Rose*. And, as I have journeyed, and as you journey with me, you will see that I too, through my life have learned much. "The Laws of the Universe," full of insights for me, will, hopefully, be insightful for you too. I would also like to share with you my own discoveries, my own personal struggle, the need for self-worth, the need for self-respect, the need for pride.

As I have traveled through my writings, Grey Eagle has been my constant companion. An Apache, a shaman, he has been a continuing source of inspiration to me. Since I began my work as

1

a spiritual medium and healer, fifteen years ago, in 1982, Grey Eagle has been my spirit guide. My teacher, my mentor . . . my best friend.

There is much to tell, and much to teach, and as Grey Eagle would say. . . . come sit with me. . . . draw close to me now. . . . past the beginning. . . . let me tell you more of my journey, of my travels to the Far East, and of how I came to America. . . . let me tell you more of the spirit world, of the earth plane. . . . of the universe and our place in it.

Come sit with me. . . . draw close to my fire. . . . warm your hands. . . . and I will continue my story.

I am a medium now, full-fledged, flying high. Having experienced so very much in the fifteen years since I began to work spiritually, I am no longer uncertain of my life. With great confidence, born of an even greater faith, I tread my path, Grey Eagle, ever watchful, by my side.

It was July 1992, and although I had never intended, indeed had never had any inclination, to visit America, there I was. It was hard to believe that just a few months before I had been in Hong Kong visiting an American friend, Lynne, and we had planned this trip.

In fact it was Lynne's suggestion that we tour the Southwest, beginning in New Mexico—Santa Fe, to be exact—and slowly working our way around to Phoenix, Arizona.

My first concern when this idea was broached was finances. Could I afford it? The answer came back loud and clear: no, I could not. But as my friend and I sat poring over the map, discussing the possible route we would take, I caught sight of the place I needed to visit—Apache Country. I looked more closely at the map. The White Mountains, Fort Apache, Apache territory, and Phoenix. I traced a line with my finger. No doubt in my mind, I heard the mountains calling me, calling me home.

This was an adventure, and I was excited. Grey Eagle was bringing me to his homeland, bringing me back.

Santa Fe was charming; Bandolier and the Frijoles Canyon, where the Anasazi Indians had lived, were incredible. The Grand Canyon was spectacular. Phoenix and our stay in a dome house . . . well, I'll tell more of these things later. But wait—let's go back to Phoenix, just for a moment, for I must recount to you my first glimpse of the mountain.

In the foyer of the hotel there were many brochures of the different places of interest, but only one caught my eye, "The Apache Trail." I picked it up and, on opening it, discovered a map. This, I was told, was where the Apache last walked free, where they hid from the soldiers, in the mountains. The trail began at the foot of Superstition Mountain, named after a Dutchman, another story, not relevant here.

I knew I had to go there, and so Lynne and I set off in our rental car to find the Apache Trail. Several times we got lost, and by the time we found the mountain, Lynne was tired and decided to curl up in the backseat and take a nap. I, on the other hand, was far from tired, and decided to explore.

I climbed out of the car into the heat and began walking up the road, which led to the foot of the mountain. All was quiet, the air still, not a soul about, not a bird nor an insect. No breeze, nothing to disturb the stillness of the day. Then, disappointment, for as I drew closer I saw that the mountain had been fenced off. It was impossible for me to go as close as I wanted.

The road bore to the right, and I continued walking, aware now of the size of the mountain, and of its voice, calling me. I looked for a place to get in, past the fence, but there was no way. Then I heard Grey Eagle's voice: "Not now, not yet. This is just the beginning, we are not ready yet. But look to the mountain, feel its strength, do not ask the reason why you are here, only be content to know that you have arrived."

I gazed at the mountain once more, then headed back to the car and to my friend, knowing I would return.

We had many experiences on this trip. It was fun, and a real adventure, as I had hoped it would be.

It was in Santa Fe, as Lynne and I sat in the lounge of our hotel having an after-dinner drink, that I came upon my first patient in America, or, more correctly, the first person I would give healing to in America. His name, if I remember correctly, was Abe. Abe and his wife were from New York and in Santa Fe for a vacation. We began chatting, and after telling us that they were in the travel business, Abe asked what I did for a living. When I mentioned that I was a healer, Abe's wife told me of her husband's serious back problem and asked if I would help.

Lynne was a little taken aback at the way the situation was progressing, but for me it was the most natural thing in the world as I sat with Abe and gave him healing by laying on hands.

> *Ask, and it shall be given unto you.*
> *Seek, and ye shall find.*

The Grand Canyon, as any of you who have experienced it will know, is a spectacle in itself, breathtaking beyond belief and, I feel, an extraordinary place where one might really sense the presence of spirit. It is, of course, the home of the Hopi Indians, and as I mention the Hopi I am reminded of a story I once heard about a journalist who was granted a rare interview with one of the Hopi elders. One of his questions to the elder was "What do you think of man's scientific achievements, such as building a rocket and sending a man to the moon?"

The Hopi elder replied, "Why would man want to build a machine to take him to the moon when he can go to the moon by himself?"

I smiled when I heard this story. Having visited the Grand

Canyon and felt the energy there I have no difficulty understanding what he means.

The dome house we stayed in was located just outside Phoenix, in a remote desert area. It belonged to a friend of Lynne's family, who had offered to put us up for a couple of nights. As we drove through the desert, along endless dusty deserted roads, our curiosity mounted. We had heard about the house, seen photographs of it, but nothing quite prepared us for the sight of it. I caught my breath as I saw the dome, huge and white, like some strange spaceship, sitting in the middle of the desert. The mountains behind made a perfect backdrop, and the way the sky seemed lit gave the scene a surreal appearance. I felt I could have walked in on the movie set of *Star Wars*.

In the middle of the second night of our stay there, Lynne woke me, saying that she could see strange lights out in the desert. I got up to take a look, and sure enough there were two bright lights, one stationary, one seeming to bob up and down. At first we tried to explain them away. Perhaps they were an airplane, but they were too low in the sky. Maybe there were people out there carrying torches, but we knew that didn't make sense either—the lights were too high in the sky for that. Eventually we gave up on ideas, and I went back to bed. Lynne, more curious than I, stayed awhile longer before she too went back to bed. We never did discover the origin of those lights. Lynne likes to think that they were alien spacecraft. Who knows? She might be right.

For me, however, the most amazing experience came as we were headed toward Phoenix. We had passed the Petrified Forest in eastern Arizona. As Lynne was the driver and I the navigator, I held the map on my knee, intent on monitoring every inch of our journey. I knew we were close to Apache territory and watched, keen-eyed, as road signs flipped past us. "About ten more minutes," I told Lynne, excitement building inside me, not knowing what to expect, expecting nothing and everything.

Then I saw it up ahead: a small and seemingly insignificant sign by the side of the road welcoming us to "Apache Country."

I pointed it out to Lynne, my voice barely above a whisper, my heart in my throat as we crossed the line. Then, without warning, something came at us, a large something, heading straight for the car. Lynne slammed the brakes on and we sat together, at first terrified and shaking, then overjoyed, as a huge eagle flew over the car's hood. We watched as this great bird soared high into the sky. As I followed its course, I saw more eagles, maybe five or six. I sat fascinated until suddenly Lynne screamed. My head snapped back to her just in time to see another eagle flying past the window, this one so close I thought it would hit us. A moment later it was gone, flying high to join the others, which were now circling overhead. Several minutes passed, and neither of us spoke until Lynne, the first to find her voice, said with great reverence and awe, "Well, Rosemary, I think that Grey Eagle has just welcomed you home."

Part I

WHAT HAPPENS
WHEN WE DIE

And so, for the time being, we will leave the mountain, we will leave the mystery, and I will attempt to answer questions that were left untouched in *The Eagle and the Rose*. It seems only fitting that I mention my first book—I hope the first of many—which elicited a tremendous response from readers worldwide. For many who read it, this book was a revelation, an awakening to the idea that there is life after death. The book triggered the beginning of some small understanding of the universe of which we are a part. Giving hope, encouragement, and enlightenment, it also awakened in many a curiosity, a need to know more.

We begin this section, as we will others, with a question to my guide, Grey Eagle, for he will travel with us on our journey through this book, and his voice will often be heard.

Question

Question: Grey Eagle, if, at death, you have wasted away due to poor health, do you cross over in this condition?

Answer: I will only tell you that each one soul is beautiful, and when soul meets soul, there is a recognition of that beauty.

What becomes important is the survival of the soul, and the retaining of the light of the soul, not the physical self, which may be old and wrinkled and wasted away.

Your concepts of beauty will differ from ours, and when you cross into the world of spirit, your true beauty ... that which lies within you ... will shine like a beacon in the night. And, like moths to a flame, those of us who will recognize beauty will draw to you.

There are those of you on the earth plane who will fear growing old. For if you have lost a loved one, you may be afraid that he or she will see you as wrinkled and aged. But when the time comes for the reuniting of two souls, the true beauty ... which is the joy of that reuniting . . . surpasses all expectation . . . and the smiles upon each face . . . radiant and at one . . . and coming together at last . . . will sweep away all fears of aging.

And when you have witnessed the joining of two hearts, there will be tears on your face which will mask your wrinkles.

And there will be laughter in the sound of your voice, which will dismiss any disfigurement you may have, and you will be made whole again . . . and the truth of who you are will be seen.

Are They
Happy?

One of the most often asked questions from those of us on this earth plane about our loved ones in the spirit world is "Are they happy?" And most of us believe, or want to believe, that they are. After all, are we not taught, certainly in the Christian faith, that when we die most of us will go to heaven, go to the light, sit at the right hand of God, and "rest in peace"? The phrase "rest in peace" is uttered at almost all funeral services in one way or another, and what it implies is happiness and contentment.

We are also taught that when we die we leave all earthly thoughts behind, that we are no longer of the earth, so therefore are unconcerned with it.

But then I say to myself, Wait a minute! Is that what I would want? When I die do I want to leave all that is of this earth behind? And what would that mean? To leave my child, my friends, all the people I care about, worry about, am concerned about? When I die and go to heaven—for heaven is surely the place I shall aim for, whatever and wherever heaven is—am I to understand that all of my caring and concerns simply evaporate as my form and state of consciousness change? Thinking of my child, I find it impossible to imagine that my deep feelings for her will alter in any way. Does "rest in peace" mean lose all earthly emotional attachment?

But I don't want to. The very thought suggests that I would become a zombie. But then again, maybe when we die there are higher issues that we have to deal with, which make it impossible and unnecessary for us to be concerned with anything other than our own spiritual growth. Maybe being with God is all-important and leaves no room for anything else.

I could go on and on, finding arguments one way, then another, as I know many do, to try to come to terms with and to understand the process of death. So for now, let us go back to the basic question "Are they happy?" and the second question, which is "Do we rest in peace?"

Having worked now as a professional medium for almost fifteen years, I have spoken with thousands of people in the spirit world. I can see them, hear them, feel them, and doing this has given me certain insights and a greater understanding of what happens to us when we die. Every one of us has the choice to step into the light, to be with God, which most of us do. But then what? What happens next? Where do we go from there? What do we become? Do we know who we are? Do we have memories? Do we have emotion? Or does the light fill us so that all we feel is light?

Well, let's start there. For most, the experience of reaching and being enveloped by the light is so overwhelming and peaceful, and the appearance of our loved ones we thought perhaps were lost to us so astounding and joyous an occasion, that any physical or emotional pain we might have had through the process of dying is forgotten, in the same way a mother forgets, the moment she holds her baby, the often terrible pain of giving birth. But after a while, when the newness of the situation has worn a little, and again, in the same way a mother remembers childbirth, the pains are gone, but the memories remain.

The mother looks at her newborn child and gladly accepts the pain, knowing that her reward is greater than the pain she suffered.

When we die, when we are reborn, we too must look to see what it is that we have gained, what our rewards are for the pains of the earth that we have surely suffered.

In a class situation a few years ago I went into trance, a state where I vacate my body and allow a spirit entity to use my empty shell. It was just before Christmas, and my students who were there that night, all of whom had witnessed trance before, were excited at the prospect of talking to Grey Eagle, or possibly to some other teacher or philosopher from the spirit world.

Full attention was given by my students now, as our visitor through trance made herself known to us. We knew her—she had been through to talk to us on a number of occasions, and always when introducing herself she would say, "I am the little old lady with no teeth."

Never having had even one glimpse of this lady, I cannot say if her physical description of herself is accurate, but within minutes of her teaching, her wisdom is so overwhelming that her physical appearance is forgotten.

As I have already said, it was less than a week until Christmas, and our teacher began the lesson by asking my students what, if she could give them a gift for Christmas, they would ask for. Their replies came slowly at first, then more confidently as each in turn gave his or her answer.

"I would ask for peace throughout the world," said one. "Peace and harmony within my family," answered another. "Healing, and the healing light, spread throughout the world," said yet another. "All wars to end." ... "Food for the starving." ... "Homes for the homeless." And so on. And in this mood, and remembering Christ and the message of love that he had given to the world, my students made their requests, all selfless, all giving and loving. Requests for peace in the spirit of Christmas.

Our teacher, the little old lady with no teeth, listened without interruption until they had finished. Then, and with a gentle voice, she replied:

"Because I am love, and come from love, and because I am your teacher, I must tell you . . . if I could give you a gift for Christmas, I would give you the gift of pain . . . I would give you the gift of heartache . . . and I would give you the gift of tears . . . for it is only through these things that you will learn, that you will grow, and that you will come to understand the nature of your soul, and of your strength."

Our teacher had, in fact, given us a gift. She had given us an insight into a most important issue, which is that we don't have to wait until we die to discover who we are, and what, as souls, we are capable of. But for many, it is only in the process of dying that we see ourselves and that we ask, "What did I gain from my earth experience? What, if any, are my rewards?" Or even, "What was the point?"

So reflecting again on the question "Are they happy?" my experience is that in certain situations, as in life on earth, many souls are not. They see themselves as having missed opportunities to grow. Many are frustrated. And yet, at the same time, they are calmed, for God's light not only shows us who we are, which we may not like to look at; it also gives us hope and enlightenment as we understand that time is on our side, that life continues and we can and will still learn.

But a large part of the frustrations of those in the spirit world has to do with us on the earth plane. They are lucky in that they have enlightenment. The very act of dying, of having had that experience and come through it, gives them knowledge they didn't have before. Dying gives them a certain amount of wisdom, which, of course, they want to impart to their loved ones, to make it easier for us. That we don't listen, or can't, or don't know how to, is their frustration. And our actions affect them, thereby creating reactions.

For instance, if a mother sees her son, emotionally depressed, going through some trauma, drinking too heavily and too often, and wrecking his life, refusing to see any light, then that mother, being a caring and loving parent, is unhappy about the situation. She is frustrated that she can do little but stand by and watch because her son cannot hear her plea that he look to the light. And even if there are many in the spirit world who tell the mother that things will be fine, that her son will find his way, she will still cry for him, for the pain that he is in, even knowing that his pain is his greatest teacher. So if this son were to ask me, "Is my mother happy now that she is with God?" I would be able to answer only that although she is in the light and is content, I see her tears, and her tears are a reaction to his actions.

Now the same mother could have a daughter. This daughter could be one who, having gone through pain and trauma, and having made a decision to walk a more spiritual path, wants to know more about her soul and is learning and growing and becoming more enlightened.

So if the daughter were to ask, "Is my mother happy?" I would be able to say, "I see your mother smiling, and happy with the way you are living your life. She feels at peace." The mother's smile is a reaction to her daughter's actions.

Basically, and perhaps seemingly too simply, what I am saying is that the state of mind, of happiness, of those in the spirit world depends to some degree on us.

Heaven is not "someplace else."

God is not "someplace else."

"The light" is not "someplace else."

Those in the spirit world are not "someplace else."

The "someplace" that heaven, and God, the light, and souls of spirit, is, is right with us, by us, part of us. And what we do affects them. And what they do affects us. For we are all . . . it is all . . . of the universe.

All those souls in the spirit world, our loved ones, are not unreachable, and certainly are not unaffected by our lives and our actions. With so much to teach us, they wait, not always patiently, for dying is not an automatic ticket to sainthood, and we retain our personalities after death. Their hope is that if they wait long enough, we who are of the earth will hear.

Questions crowd my mind . . . and I listen as my guide gives me aid to discover my answers.

What is heaven?

According to *Webster's Dictionary,* heaven is the abode of the Deity, and of the blessed dead. A place of supreme happiness. Other names for heaven are Olympus; Valhalla; Asgard; Elysian Fields; Elysium; Happy Hunting Ground; Earthly Paradise; Eden or Garden of Eden; Garden of the Hesperides; Islands of the Blest; and in fantasy, Isle of Avalon.

Grey Eagle's answer when I ask what is heaven is simply . . . place of light.

When we die, what do we become?

We become more, and more enlightened.

Do we know who we are, who we were on earth?

We retain all knowledge, all memory, all learning. We retain our personality, and have opportunities to improve if we so desire. As for the first part of this question . . . do we know who we are . . . well, this is what our quest is all about, this is what the soul wishes to discover. And our journey on the earth plane certainly gives us insights into the true nature of the self.

Do we have emotion?

Without emotion we are nothing, for what is love but a heart-felt emotion? And we each of us who are of God are love, are emotion.

And are they happy now?

They are content.

These, my questions, these, my answers. And I feel Grey Eagle's hand on my shoulder in acknowledgment of my learning. I smile . . . my acknowledgment of his teaching.

✧　✧　✧

Earlier in this chapter, I mention how when we die, when we are reborn, we must look to see what we gained from the experience of our earth journey, and what our reward is for the pains we suffered on that journey. So many religions focus upon rewards and punishments after we die, and in doing this have forced us to concentrate more on what is in heaven rather than what is on earth, as if the two things were separate.

And then there are those of us who, not totally discarding our orthodox religions, try to absorb what is commonly called "New Age material," more enlightened spiritual teachings. When I walk into a bookstore I am always amazed at the amount of literature in the New Age section, my own book included. And I always smile when I see or hear this literature referred to as "New Age," when these teachings are as old as man, and older than man, as old as the universe of which we are a part.

We all talk about "going to the light," being "embraced by the light," "finding the light," "looking to the light," etc. But what so many of us don't realize is that we *are* the light. Each of us *is* light. The human race—every animal, every insect, every tree and every plant, every living thing—is light, and is of the light. We do not have to look out into space, heavenward, to find God in his heaven. We do not have to wait until we die to experience heaven, to experience light ... "the light." For every day we have that experience, with ourselves, with each other, with the spirit world, and with God, who is light, and all we have to do is recognize it.

I would like to tell you a story of a lady who was so obsessed with heaven, believing it to be anywhere other than where she was, that for almost fifty years she lived in darkness. We will call her Mrs. Lennox. Mrs. Lennox was a war bride. She met and married her husband within five days. She was twenty-six years old. Less than two weeks after they were married, her husband, John, was called back to his barracks. He was in the Air Force, a gunner, and when Mrs. Lennox waved goodbye to him she did not realize she would never see him again. His plane was shot down just days after his return and all on board were killed.

Nine months later, a child was born, a girl, and Mrs. Lennox named her Patricia. Years passed. Forty years. And Patricia grew into a fine young woman, was married, and eventually had children of her own, three boys. Mrs. Lennox should have been happy; she should have been thrilled that this one child could reap such bounties in which she could share.

But Mrs. Lennox was not a happy person. Ever since she was widowed she had mourned her husband with outstanding fervor. She had reproduced their wedding photograph and the one photograph she had of him on his own in his uniform, and had placed them all around the house. Her entire life had been spent worshiping this man she hardly knew, and every morning and every evening she would pray to God to take her to him. She would beat her breast and tear her hair, weeping and wailing, bemoaning her loss and the fact she was a widow, struggling to bring up a child on her own.

Every day she looked heavenward, searching, seeking, calling his name, always believing he could hear her, see her. Refusing any other man even the smallest part of her life, she clung to her husband with a zeal that blotted out any other life, or light.

Then she heard of me. Now into her seventies, Mrs. Lennox came to me for a consultation. I knew nothing of her story, and when immediately upon sitting down she told me the only person she wanted to speak to was her husband, I saw nothing unusual about this.

I saw him straightaway, and I was pleased that we had been able to make such a good connection. He told me how he had been killed during the war, and as I recounted this to Mrs. Lennox I was also able to describe the uniform he wore, and how he had looked in his early thirties, with brown eyes and dark hair.

She became very excited and told me how long she had waited for this moment. Smiling my delight at her obvious pleasure, I turned back to John Lennox, expecting to continue the session. Imagine my surprise when in a voice gruff with irritation he said, "Okay, I've given her my name, rank, and number. Now will you tell her to go away and leave me alone?"

I was stunned. Never had I had this happen before. Looking at Mrs. Lennox, who, totally unaware of this new situation, was watching me with a sort of suspenseful excitement, I knew I was in trouble. I turned back to Mr. Lennox. "Please," I said, "can't you talk to her a little more? She has waited so long for this, and she knows now that you are here. If I tell her you don't want to talk to her, it will hurt her so."

"For over forty years this woman has been pulling at me, tugging at me, calling out to me for help, not once thinking to help herself. In the beginning I tried, but I refuse to say more to a woman who is a stranger to me, and who I have watched wallow in self-pity, wasting her life and her lessons," he replied. "The only reason I have come today is because she is the mother of my child, and all my love is for my daughter." With that John Lennox turned his back and refused to say a further word.

There was no way I could repeat these things to Mrs. Lennox— she would have been too hurt. As it was, she was hurt enough when I simply said I had lost the connection and must end the session.

Although I never saw Mrs. Lennox again, several weeks later I had another visit from Mr. Lennox, and a visit that was far removed from the last one.

His daughter came to see me. Having heard from her mother that as a medium I was not much good, but from others how good I was, Patricia Lennox decided she would see for herself. This time there was no reticence on her father's part. Very quickly John Lennox let his daughter know that he had been following her progress through life since she was a baby. He wanted to let her know how proud he was of her success despite her mother's possessiveness and narrowness.

When Patricia heard this she broke down and cried. She told me how difficult it had been for her growing up—how, when she reached her teenage years, her mother had been determined to control her life. "She had no life of her own," said Patricia, "and so she wanted control of mine. I have truly prayed that she could be happy, but I know she never will be."

How wonderful that John Lennox and his daughter found each other, found and gave love to each other. And how sad that his wife not only wasn't welcome in his life, but had had no life of her own to speak well of.

Had she known the consequences of her actions, would she have acted differently? I like to think so. I would like to think that had she understood that he needed her to live her life to the fullest, to find happiness, so that he would be free to get on with his life, she would have made more effort with her life, if not for her sake, then for his.

Are they happy now? There's that question again. John Lennox was not happy with his wife but was ecstatic with his daughter. Their successes, their failures, their actions, created in him varying reactions, determining to some extent his state of well-being.

We on this earth have a responsibility to our loved ones in the spirit world, to our loved ones on this earth, and to ourselves. But if we truly wish happiness for our loved ones in the spirit world, then no matter how difficult it is, we must try to ensure that each step through life we take is a good one, a positive one—that each act we perform is an act of light, an act of love. To remember that heaven is not "someplace else" but in our hearts and minds, and all around us. For we are light, and as our light grows brighter with this knowledge, then the light of all God's creatures, all beings, will embrace us, as surely as we embrace them.

This responsibility is a heavy one, not easy to carry, and we will often let our loved ones and ourselves down. Grey Eagle teaches me . . . it does not matter if you fail, and if you fail again . . . it only matters that you try.

Ghost Story

This story I am now about to recount is very different from the last, but will illustrate, in another way, how easy it can often be to create unhappiness in our lives. We cling through fear to what we know or desire, rather than accepting reality and moving forward.

How do I begin?—I'm not sure yet—but I know I must try. For this is a story about what happens when someone dies, but refuses to accept death . . . and the light. I cannot tell you where it happened, only that it was in America, somewhere on the East Coast. I cannot give you real names, only substitutes, in order to protect certain persons. Still, there is a danger they may be recognized.

This, I suppose, is where my skills as a writer must show themselves. Difficult, for as my friend and editor Joann knows, I have never claimed to be a writer, merely a teller of stories—true stories.

Lobster is a favorite with me, but I had eaten it only in restaurants until this night. I had been invited with my friend Ellen to the home of Ruth and Jo, a couple who had been most caring and helpful to me with, and prior to, the publication of my first book, *The Eagle and the Rose*. They knew of my love of lobster, and I sat now with them at their table, my hands, almost to my wrists—I'm a very messy eater at times—were covered with clarified butter and lobster juices—oh so good. But what was even better was the conversation. The subject . . . ghosts. And Ruth began the story.

Her company owned a vast amount of real estate. Its office was set among acres of land with beautiful gardens, and part of the property was a large house—a mansion, actually—which had once belonged to a well-known and very wealthy American family. It is this property and this family on which our story centers.

Ruth, who held a major position with the company, had access to the house, which had a large ballroom and was used for various functions and parties. Occasionally people from outside the company would rent the place, since it was ideal for summer balls and Christmas parties. And the house was haunted, or so the story goes.

In the early part of the century, the daughter of the house was married, a happy affair. The young couple were very much in love. They were on their honeymoon in Pennsylvania when they were given the news. It had been discovered that the bridegroom was a second or third cousin to the bride. This discovery so devastated the bride that she hanged herself, and the story is told that she went back to her home, where she wandered, a lost and suffering specter, for years. Apparently there had been many sightings of this "ghost" and countless reports of strange and uncanny happenings at the house. As my evening with Ruth and Jo progressed, I found myself intrigued by the "ghost" and her sad story, and I wondered if, supposing the story was true (and many ghost stories are not), I could do anything to help her.

As I voiced my interest, to my delight Ruth suggested that I could visit the house. "If you are really interested," she said, "I'm sure I can arrange it."

A few days later I found myself riding with Ellen in her car through the estate. The grounds were large, and we were lost. Then the car, which had behaved perfectly up to this point, suddenly cut out. We were stranded. What were we to do? We climbed out of the car and looked around. All we could see was open ground, beautiful gardens which seemed to stretch for miles. No buildings, no people.

Just as we were beginning to despair, however, around a curve in the road came a small blue security car. The driver, a security guard, seeing us there, had come to the rescue. We explained that we were to meet Ruth at the house. He assumed that we were interested in renting the house and offered to take us there. We climbed into his car, and for all our mishaps so far, we still arrived a little early.

The house was huge and imposing, but the day was warm and sunny and it was hard to imagine that anyone could find this place "spooky." While we waited for Ruth to arrive I engaged our guard in conversation, asking him if he was familiar with the house at all. He looked at me a little strangely and asked what I meant by that. "Well," I said, "have you ever heard anyone mention that the house might be haunted?"

He looked sideways at me for a moment. There was more than a trace of apprehension in his face as he said tentatively, "There have been rumors." But some instinct told me he knew more than he was saying, so I pressed on.

He was a tall man, tough and hard-looking, standing there in the sunlight in his uniform, muscles bulging through his shirt. His black skin shone with health. He wore a gun on one hip, a truncheon and a large bunch of keys on the other. It was hard to imagine that this man would be afraid of anything.

"Well," he began, as I pressed further, "I've heard some stories from the other guards. One or two won't come down here after dark. They say the lights go on and off, and they've heard strange wailing noises coming from the house." Still I knew he wasn't telling all, and I nudged him a little more. "Have you had any experience yourself?" I asked innocently, knowing that he had, but not knowing what it was.

He looked down at the ground, shuffling his feet, trying to decide if he could tell me, not wanting to appear a fool. "You might think I'm making it up," he eventually said. Then, more defiantly, "But I'm not."

I looked at him and smiled. "No, I won't," I replied. "Why don't you tell me about it?"

"Well," he said, a little sheepishly now, "I won't go in the place if I can help it. About two years ago I decided to go on upstairs, back there"—he gestured back toward the house. "Lots of guys swore it was haunted, said they had seen things, so I decided to take a look for myself. I got as far as the second floor. At the top of the stairs, down the hallway, there is an old refectory table. It was covered with dust. When I got right up to it I noticed, written in the dust, in large bold letters, the words 'GET OUT.'

"Well," he continued, "That's just what I did. I turned and ran for the stairs so fast I tripped on the top step and came down those stairs facedown. It felt like the devil was after me, and I tell you, I ain't been back in there since. I just check on the locks and hope the alarm doesn't go off."

I listened, nodding. When he had finished his story I told him that I wanted to go inside myself. The guard, Bill, had told me I couldn't go in without an escort. Ruth was late, and for some reason I didn't want to wait.

"What if you took me in?" I said. Then, placing my hand on the big man's arm in a reassuring gesture, I said gently, "It's okay. I'll look after you. You'll be safe with me." And to his surprise, he meekly nodded his agreement.

My friend Ellen decided she would rather wait outside in the sunshine for Ruth, so Bill and I entered the house by ourselves. "Let's go upstairs first," I said, and without resistance, he followed as I headed up.

I went from room to room, watching, listening, looking for signs. If there was a lost soul in here, maybe I could find her, maybe I could help . . . if she would allow me to.

Bill followed me around, careful to keep two paces away from me. His suspicions that I was not here to rent a room were growing as he watched me. Up more stairs we went, into more rooms, but there was no sign of her. As Bill spoke, however, tentatively asking what I was doing, I became aware of the man walking with him. A father figure, I knew, but not his father. This man, whose words as yet were unheard by his "son," told me he had died of a sudden and massive heart attack.

"You're looking for ghosts, aren't you?" Bill asked. Then, without waiting for a reply, he said, "You believe in this stuff, don't you?"

"Yes, Bill," I replied softly, knowing that it was no coincidence that he was here with me now. "And I believe in the man I see standing beside you, your true father, even though he is not tied to you in blood."

Bill nodded, accepting totally, unsurprised and only grateful at his "father's" appearance. "I know that he's around me. I feel his presence often," he said. And it was as simple as that.

We had now entered a room, the only room that was carpeted, and together we sat down on the floor. For the next forty minutes I spoke with the one man in Bill's life whom he had truly loved.

"He is telling me first about your childhood," I began. And with that, as in a vision, I saw Bill's life played out before me. I saw how as a child, if he misbehaved, he would be locked up in a small cupboard and left there for hours as punishment. I saw how as a young man growing up in a painful and difficult environment, he had struggled with his emotions, how he had become in some ways mentally crippled by the treatment he had received as a boy. I learned of his search to find peace, how he had sought help from priests and psychologists in an attempt to understand the cruel disciplines his parents had inflicted upon him as a child. I saw and heard, and listened further as his "father" then recounted the story of how Bill had eventually met and fallen in love with his wife, who had been able to help him achieve self-esteem and self-worth.

I had communicated all of this to Bill, of course. Then his "father" said, "Tell Bill I've seen the baby, his son." And if that small piece of information was not enough to startle him, the next certainly was. "And tell him I like his wife. She's pretty, but boy, did she get some haircut! So short there's almost no hair left." Bill's "father" said this with a chuckle. But Bill was so stunned he leaped up, flew to the far side of the room, and stood there shaking his head from side to side, repeating over and over, "How did you know that? How did you know that?"

Understanding his reaction, I patted the floor next to me and said, "Come and sit down here, Bill. Please don't be afraid. Your 'father' only wants you to know he's alive and still close to you, still interested and involved in your life."

Bill came and sat down next to me, still a little shaken, but much comforted by what I had just said. Then, for the next fifteen minutes, Bill's father talked to Bill, through me. He spoke about Bill's night school classes and his determination to succeed in life, and about how his childhood experiences, difficult as they had been, had served as lessons, making him strong, helping him understand that he could survive in life, be a success, if he worked hard, and that he had within him the strength to surmount all odds. Bill had never looked at it that way before. But now, as his "father" spoke of his love for his "son," he felt oddly comforted. Tears rained down his face, love for this man who was his true father spilling forth. Taking my hands, quietly, and with tremendous humility, he thanked me for the gift that I had given him.

Now, as if on cue, my friends Ellen and Ruth stood in the open doorway. They were somewhat startled to find me sitting on the floor with the security guard. Taking charge, I stood up and said hello as if my position were the most natural in the world. I smiled at them, saying, "I'm all done up here, I think. Perhaps we should go and have a look on the ground floor."

And with that we all headed down the stairs, Bill walking closely by my side, now my own personal bodyguard. He was to tell me later that all the psychiatrists, therapists, priests, and others he had been to over the years had not been able, collectively, to give him what I had been able to give him . . . peace.

But back to the "ghost hunt."

First, as we reached the ground floor, I went into what had originally been the ballroom, now used for banquets and company functions. Nothing there. I could feel no vibration that would indicate to me that the place was "haunted." Then I crossed the hallway to another large room, which had been turned into a lecture room. Chairs were placed in rows, facing a blackboard, and next to this was a movie screen on a tripod. I looked around and felt and saw nothing unusual, and so I headed back into the hall. The staircase was impressive, the ceilings high, and the thought came to me that in its day this must have been a gracious house.

It was as I turned to go back into the lecture room that I heard the rustle of her skirts and, turning back toward the foot of the stairs and looking up, I saw her. She was regal and beautiful, her head up, shoulders back. Her left hand resting lightly on the banister, she looked down at me. There was no welcoming smile on her lips; her eyes were hard and staring. Without saying one word she let me know that I was an intruder in her home. She didn't want me there.

I understood immediately. She knew the reason I was there, that I intended, if I could, to help her, perhaps to persuade her to move on, and she was afraid. She had spent so much time in the house, her home, where she had grown up, where there were happy memories. This was where she wanted to stay, and she saw me as a threat to that, a stranger, meddling in her life, a life, no matter how narrow, she had chosen to live.

With great compassion I smiled up at her. "Please let me help you," I said. I spoke these words silently. Neither Ellen, nor Ruth, nor Bill heard me, or even knew that I had seen the "ghost."

"Go away!" she shouted back at me. "Go away and leave me be. I'm happy here, I am, I am." She spoke with desperation, as if trying to convince herself as well as me.

Again I spoke. "It can't be much fun for you here on your own. It would be so easy, and so much better, if you could move on. Why don't you let me help?" I said, careful to keep my voice low, so I wouldn't alarm her further. But she shook her head violently, determined not to listen to anything I had to say. Sadly I turned away and headed back into the lecture room.

Ruth and Ellen had wandered off, Ruth showing Ellen around a little. My guard stayed close to my side, and when I sat in one of the chairs he came and sat down next to me.

What was I to do? Our "ghost"—I'll call her Sarah, for she was no more a ghost to me than you or I, just a person in distress—was obviously in no mood to talk to me. She was trapped here in this house, had been trapped for more than thirty years, but her incarceration had been voluntary. Having "died," she was in such emotional turmoil that she had turned away from the light, had chosen to remain earthbound, and had returned, like a child, to the only safe place she knew.

I must point out at this juncture, for the benefit of those readers who have lost a loved one to suicide, and who are now perhaps concerned about that loved one's transition, that although Sarah's position is not a unique one, this situation occurs only very, very infrequently. In my last book I dedicated a whole chapter to the subject of suicide. It is my opinion, based on years of experience, that the chance of someone getting "lost," refusing to meet and embrace the loved ones in the spirit world who are always waiting and ready to help as we pass into our next/continuing life, is so minimal as to be virtually nonexistent.

And so back to Sarah, and to my dilemma. What to do?

As I sat pondering this, I felt Grey Eagle draw close to me. "You have been brought here, child, to help. Be patient and trust."

As I listened to my guide I sat with my head down. Now... "Lift up your head, little one, there is someone here who wishes to speak to you."

Slowly I lifted my head, assured now that help was at hand. As I looked, my eyes were drawn to the screen that sat on a tripod next to the blackboard. I smiled, for there, almost as if I were watching a slide show, I saw a man, or more accurately, I saw his face, enlarged and in perfect focus. He smiled back at me and gave his name. I'll call him Eric. "I 'died' a few weeks ago," he told me. "A heart attack, very quick, not too surprising as I'm getting on in years. It's good of you to come," he continued, "for you see, I need your help, we need your help, my family and I. My parents have tried everything, they have called and called, but she has refused to listen or even acknowledge our existence, or rather their existence. Now I'm here, and she does acknowledge me. We were always very close, but still she's afraid to let go. You see, Rosemary, I love her very much. Your ghost, my Sarah ...she's my sister."

Later I spoke to Ruth about Eric, and she confirmed that he had once been the owner of the house. Eric was a writer, the author of many books. He had died of a heart attack just a few weeks before.

As I listened to Eric I felt saddened by his story and immediately asked what I could do.

"We would like you to have a party," he replied, "just a small affair. We'd like him to come," pointing to Bill, "and those two," indicating Ellen and Ruth, who had at that moment walked into the room, and pointing directly at Ruth, "and her husband, and of course, Rosemary," this next said with a small chuckle, "we would like you to come too. Bring drinks and food please, a small picnic." Then he added, "I know my request sounds odd, but if you could just humor me I would be grateful."

I asked Eric when he would like us to come back—tomorrow

perhaps, or later in the week? "No," he said, "tonight would be best." And when I asked him what time, as in all the best ghost stories, you will not be surprised when I tell you he said midnight.

I relayed now to Bill, Ruth, and Ellen all that I had seen and heard, finishing by inviting them to the party. They were at first a little apprehensive about returning, but then intrigued, and concerned for Sarah.

We relied on Bill to arrive first and unlock the house once again, but we all, including Ruth's husband, Jo, turned up at the same time, saving Bill the embarrassment of having to admit that he was too nervous to enter the house on his own.

To set the scene I have to tell you that, yes, it was a full moon. The sky was clear, the stars bright, but there was no wind—indeed the night was very still.

We walked into the house, everyone behind, me leading, and found our way into the ballroom, where Eric had told me to go. Although there were lights in the house I had decided to keep the ballroom lights off. Bill and Jo rounded up some chairs, and soon we were seated at the end of the huge room, in a circle, with a small hamper filled with sodas and cheese and crackers placed in the middle on the floor. Moonlight shone through the windows and bathed the room in a soft glow. Light also filtered in from the hall, so we could see quite clearly.

"What do we do now?" whispered Ellen nervously. I had already told them what they might expect, but also made it clear that nothing at all might happen. I had also explained that it was important that no matter what happened, no matter what they saw or heard, they were to keep perfectly calm and trust me to know what I was doing. This last request was easy for them to grant, as they had all, at different times, been recipients of my gift of mediumship.

I patted Ellen's hand in reassurance. "We wait," I replied, "but stay aware. Let me know if you see or hear anything." Then I added with a smile, "And don't be scared. *I'm* here."

Silence, silence. And as the minutes ticked by, still more silence. It had been almost midnight when we sat down, and as a distant church clock struck the hour my guests had looked to me with certainty that something now would happen, for in all good ghost stories the "witching hour" features strongly. But still we waited, and still I looked, searching for, asking for, Eric.

Grey Eagle was by my side, and having been in similar circumstances before, I was prepared to wait.

At least fifteen minutes went by before I saw him. He had brought a number of others with him. Friends and family, I gathered. He too had brought guests to the party. He smiled and said hello, said that he was pleased we were here. Then I noticed the woman who stood, shyly and a little nervously, by his side. The same woman I had seen on the stairs, Sarah, our ghost.

Tentatively she pointed toward Ruth and Jo. "They were at my Christmas party this year, and last year too," she said softly.

As I recounted this, Ruth and Jo nodded. "It was the company's Christmas party," said Ruth.

"It was no such thing," said Sarah indignantly. "It was *my* party, this is *my* house, and you were *my* guests." Then, more gently and a little shyly, she reached out and touched Jo's hair. "He kept the fires going," she said. "He admired my fireplaces, and all night long he tended the fires, placing logs on them, keeping them alight. I watched him. I like him, and I'm pleased he has come to the party tonight."

Jo was amazed when he heard this, and verified that he had done just that. "The fireplaces are so beautiful. It was a pleasure to see them lit," he said.

Then Sarah said, pointing to Ruth, "I've seen her in the schoolroom often, and I have often sat in on her lectures." In a thoughtful voice, she added, "I think she's quite good."

Ruth laughed at this and said she hoped that was the opinion of her bosses.

It was a revelation to them that they had been observed when in the house—Bill too, along with all the other security guards who had kept watch over the building. Sarah recounted more details of their comings and goings.

After a while I became aware of a man and woman standing close to Jo. Grey Eagle told me they were his family, come to say hello, and to talk to him. This was a moving experience for all of us, for as these two from the spirit world gave evidence of their survival to Jo, they recounted stories of Jo's childhood, which had been very similar to Bill's and just as painful. Jo, in tears and remembering, admitted that this had affected his life, that he found it hard as an adult to shake the feeling of low self-esteem. But as often happens when those from the spirit world come and talk to us, many issues were cleared up, many explanations and apologies given. Most important, his family, these two people, sick at heart for the pain that had been caused to Jo as a boy, sent him their love and told him they were with him, and a great healing took place.

Someone handed Jo a tissue, and pretty soon we were all wiping our eyes, pleased for Jo as he told us he felt a great weight had been lifted from his shoulders.

Relieved by this, I looked once again to Eric. He was standing next to his sister, who now looked relaxed. The tension I had seen earlier in her face was now gone, and she looked from her brother to me, her smile warm and easy.

"It's time," Eric said, placing his arm around his sister's shoulders. Then, pointing to the hamper, he said to me, "Sarah would like you to eat and drink with us, for we are celebrating her release from pain, her release from this house, and from the earth plane." Hugging her tight to him, and with tears in his eyes, he said softly, "She's coming with me." Standing upright and taking a deep breath, he smiled at me. "This will be her—our—last party in this house. You will be our last guests. After this night we will never visit here again." Looking to Sarah again, he whispered,

"We're going home, to the light, and to our family, who are waiting."

I relayed all this to Bill, Jo, Ruth, and Ellen, and then, respectful of the occasion, and with quiet dignity, we reached into the hamper, took out our sodas and crackers, and drank a toast to Sarah and Eric and their new life.

I heard her laughing, and I heard the rustle of her skirts as her brother danced her around the room for the last time. Strains of music, Chopin I think, floated through the air, but were heard only by me and those in the spirit world. Then again I heard her laughter, the laughter of someone who is totally happy. And I knew that she was finally free.

It was time to go, and so I told the others. Quietly we put away the chairs and packed up the hamper. Then, silently, we headed for the door. As we filed out, not one of us spoke, each believing that everything that needed to be said had been said, all of us feeling a sense of peace and accomplishment. The door closed, Bill checked the alarm and turned the key, and we walked toward our cars.

First Bill hugged me, then Jo and Ruth, and we said our good-byes...and a small breeze came up...and a sound, like sweet music on the wind...and Sarah's voice...goodbye...goodbye ...goodbye...goodbye.

And the moon shone bright, bathing us all in light....

Karma

Do animals survive?

This is one of the most common questions I am asked, and although I addressed it briefly in *The Eagle and the Rose*, when I told the story of the man who came through from the spirit world carrying two live geese, I thought it would be good to share with you some other animal stories.

The answer to the question is yes. Animals, pets we have loved, have had a special relationship with, do survive death. Often, either in a private consultation or at a lecture, I will see animals. They will be brought into the communication often by a close relative or friend. I was once at a bookstore signing in Danbury, Connecticut, and gave a woman there a message that her prize horse, whom she adored and who had died tragically earlier that year, was safe and well.

Then, of course, I have many clients who have lost pets. One client in particular comes to mind. When she rang to make an appointment, she asked if it would be possible for me to make contact with her little dog, Susie, who had died just a few weeks before. This was her sole purpose in visiting me, because, she said, her dogs were everything to her—they were her family. When she came for her consultation, not only did I see Susie, who, being a small dog, was carried by my client's grandmother, I was also shown a garden, a place where trees and plants and beautiful flowers grew. And in this garden I saw many animals—dogs, cats, rabbits, etc.—playing together and happy. I was able to tell my client that Susie often walked in this garden, played with the other animals, and was happy.

A friend and student of mine, Joan Carter, lost her little Yorkshire terrier and was heartbroken. One day two or three weeks later, as we sat in class and were just about to begin the lesson, I looked up from the folder that sat on my knee to see this little dog, healthy and happy, sitting on my friend's shoulder, just as he used to do before he died. Joan was thrilled when I told her. The knowledge that he was safe helped her in her grief.

But perhaps the best example I can offer is of my own experience of losing and then being reunited with my beloved pets. To do that I would ask that you bear with me, for I would like to tell this story from its beginning.

Karma died on June 1, 1994. As I buried him in the ground, under a huge rhododendron with enormous white blossoms, memories of our first meeting came to me. It was fourteen years ago, and my daughter, Samantha, then twelve and a half years old, had begged and pleaded for a dog, a King Charles Cavalier, a black-and-tan. She had been very specific about the breed and color, but although I had scoured the country, I could not find a kennel that had what we wanted. Furthermore, each time I had asked Grey Eagle for help, he showed me a picture of a puppy with long pale beige ears.

Well, I'm sure you know what's coming next. When all seemed lost and no puppies were to be found, I called the last kennel on the list. No, they couldn't help, but wait a moment—they knew of a woman who occasionally had litters. She didn't have a kennel, she bred from home. They gave me her name—Rix, Mrs. Rix— but they didn't have her phone number. When I heard the name

I connected it immediately with a client of mine. Could it be the same one? A long shot, but worth a try.

I looked it up in my files, found the phone number, and dialed. I spoke to a young girl who said she was Marie Rix's daughter, and I tentatively asked if they were the Rixes who bred King Charles Cavaliers. "Yes," she said. "We've got a litter now, three bitches and one dog." I said I'd call later, and could she tell her mum that I was very interested in the dog. "Oh, yes," I breathed, and asked the question I already knew the answer to: "What color are they?"

"Blenheim," replied the girl. "White and beige."

Marie Rix brought the pup to see us later that day. He was just two weeks old, so tiny he fitted into the palm of my hand. He was lively and wriggling, but when I placed him instinctively in the crook of my neck, he curled up and fell fast asleep.

Marie smiled. "We think we choose the dog," she said, "but in reality it is they who choose, and I think, Rosemary, that he just chose you."

Samantha was delighted and couldn't wait for the day we could bring him home. Four weeks later, Marie Rix called to tell us we could fetch him, two weeks earlier than we had originally planned. "He's driving his sisters crazy, chasing their tails and generally making a nuisance of himself," she laughed. "And quite frankly you might find him a bit of a handful."

But I was not worried. After all, Grey Eagle had guided me to this pup—I felt sure of that. And so, nuisance or not, it was meant to be.

I named him Karma, from the Hindu word which means the force generated by a person's actions, or, as some might say, the life's breath. Force, energy, vibration, breath—whatever it is called, I felt that that force, that energy, was in part this small puppy, meant for me.

When he was not quite one year old I decided that he needed a companion, a playmate, and so I looked around and, with much less difficulty this time, found Jasper, another King Charles Cavalier. They instantly became friends, and I watched for the next three years as they grew and played together.

Although they were the same breed, it was amazing to me how different in character they were. Jasper was the lively, bouncy one, always ready to bound up onto my lap the moment I sat down, Karma, after his lively puppy days, was more somber, a gentle and calm little dog.

When Jasper was two and a half and Karma a year older, I knew one of my boys was going to die. I was talking about them one day to a friend when I saw a vision, or rather more accurately, a picture, the spirit of Jasper, making its way heavenward. I was, of course, upset by the image. I asked Grey Eagle for more information, thinking that Jasper's death might be prevented if I could just know the circumstances, but I received no more details. I knew that what I had seen was one of life's inevitables.

However, hope lives eternal. Three months later, having caught and shaken to death a huge rat he had found in my orchard garden, Jasper had a major hemorrhage and almost died. (We discovered later that the rat had eaten some kind of poison.) I convinced myself this must be it, this must have been what I'd seen.

Two months later, when we had had bad storms and high winds, part of the fencing in the garden became dislodged, leaving a gap at the bottom, small enough to go unnoticed by me, but just big enough for an inquisitive little animal like Jasper to squeeze through. He ran out onto the road and straight in front of a truck.

The truck driver slammed on his brakes too late to avoid him, and Jasper lived just long enough to be placed into my arms, to hear my voice, soft and gentle, telling him I loved him. He looked at me one last time, then I saw his eyes glaze over. He took a deep breath, sighed, and was gone. My heart broken, I cried for days, and for many weeks, even months, every time we came into the house, Karma would race around, upstairs and downstairs, searching for his friend.

I had searched too, but in a different way, looking to see if I could catch a glimpse of Jasper in the spirit world. It was several months before I did so, and then it was quite unexpected. It was morning. Karma was sitting on the bed with me and I was about to get up when I felt something cold and wet on the back of my neck. Startled, I turned to see what it was, and saw Jasper, quite clearly. He put his nose into my hair, sniffing and pushing as he used to do. I felt his breath, and smelled him, and I saw Karma's reaction too. His tail was wagging nineteen to the dozen, and he was crying with excitement. For maybe ten minutes we were three together again, my boys and I. Then, just as quickly as he had come, my Jasper went again.

Often since that time over the years I glimpsed him and knew that he was safe and happy. I never got another dog, although I thought about it from time to time, but I felt that Karma was content, and so for the next ten years he was my only faithful companion.

As Karma grew older, his joints became stiff, he developed a heart murmur, and he became a bit of a creaking gate with a few aches and pains. But he was always, even in pain, a loving soul, a gentle-natured little boy.

Many times through the years I gave him healing. Not surprisingly, he was a very psychic little animal and would often, for no apparent reason, suddenly sit up and stare hard, either at the ceiling or in the corners of the room, his head moving sharply from place to place as if he were following some movement. People who didn't know us would find this quite unnerving, but I would smile and reassure them that it was only a visitor for Karma.

The last few months of his life he became more and more sick. His lungs had filled with fluid and his heart was weak. Each day, and several times a day, I gave him healing, which always calmed and comforted him. As always I would feel the centers of my palms grow warm and begin to throb, a sign that my energy was flowing, flowing from me to my little boy.

Karma was not a particularly pretty animal. He was cross-eyed, he smelled dreadful as he got older, and his hair came out in patches. But he was a gentle and loving little dog, and very special to me and to Samantha. When he became sick it was a comfort to me that in some small way, by placing my hands on him and using my energy, combined with God's energy, which I prayed for, I was able to ease his pain.

As you read this, I know that many of you who are animal lovers and have had sick pets, are wishing that in some way you too had the ability to give healing. And not just those of you who have animals, but those who have a loved one sick and in pain.

It is my belief that we all, to some degree, have the gift to heal, that we are born with that gift. When a child falls and grazes its knee, instinctively we gather up the child and, placing our hands on the injured spot, say, "Let me rub it better." If we have a headache, again, instinctively, our hands go to our brow and we may gently massage our temples. We have an innate ability, born to us, to give—by touch, by energy—healing. In my next book, titled *You Own the Power*, I will talk more of this and show how, by using simple exercises, we can develop this gift to some degree.

Eventually there came the day, that day which all of us who love our animals dread. It was time to make the final decision, one which I had prayed I would not have to make. It was not a surprise to me that Karma was dying, for Grey Eagle had warned me in advance, as he had with Jasper, and even given me the month. Again it was as in a vision that I saw my boy, lying, as if sleeping, outside on the grass, the sun bright, the month June.

I had seen this vision just less than one year before. Now here it was the beginning of June, and Karma had taken a distinct turn for the worse. I knew it had to be today. He couldn't lie down, he could hardly sit, and only managed to do so by propping himself against a wall. And when I looked at him I saw it in his eyes, his pleading: "Do something, help me."

As I dialed the number my heart felt leaden. How was I going to do this? I asked myself. Those of you who have been in a similar situation will know: you find the strength in love.

I took him out with me into the garden and laid him on my knee, my arms around him as I sat on the grass. When the vet brought the needle close to him I had one crazy moment when I wanted to shout out, "*No, no!*" But I bit my lip, and as tears coursed their way down my cheeks, I held my Karma more tightly to me, whispering lovingly to him. I watched as he died in my arms.

I didn't hear the vet leave—a friend had come, and had shown her out. I sat in quiet solitude for quite some time, not yet wanting to let go of this little animal who had been my friend for thirteen years.

Finally I laid him down, knowing that I must now take him to his most favorite place, the woods he loved to roam in, and bury him under the big white-blossomed rhododendron. As I returned to carry him to the car, I stopped and looked at him as he lay, seemingly peacefully asleep on the grass, and the vision Grey Eagle had given the year before came fully back to me, and I was comforted by the fact that it had been his time.

The house was now so empty. Samantha had left home two years earlier, and now my dog was gone. Each night I went to bed with my heart aching, for as smelly and mangy as he had been in his latter years, Karma always slept next to my bed, and my last act at bedtime was to stroke him and say good night.

On the third night, in the middle of the night, I woke, turned over, and, as always, reached my hand down to the side of the bed to give Karma a reassuring pat. As I stroked him I murmured the usual love phrases: "It's all right, little boy, I'm here," and

"Try and sleep now, I'll give you healing," and "Yes, yes, you're my beautiful boy."

It was only after several minutes that, realizing Karma was gone, I fully woke. With a start I sat up in bed, my hand, the hand I had been stroking Karma with, frozen in midair. And there I saw him, sitting upright by the side of the bed, half leaning against it as he always did. I reached out my hand to him and felt him under me, firm and solid, the hair on his head soft as silk through my fingers. He half turned his head and gazed at me, a contented look on his face. His breathing was strong and even, his breath warm and sweet.

One more time I stroked him, telling him as I did so that I loved my little boy. Then, a smile on my face, knowing my Karma had arrived safely and was happy, I lay down again and went to sleep.

The question? Do animals survive after death?

Well, as you can see from reading my story, yes...I believe they do.

Another Life

I lay in the coffin, terrified, screaming, but hearing no sound, recognized the sound was in my head.

Frantic, hardly able to breathe, I began to claw the lid. A futile act, but one I must perform, for I could not just be still and die, even knowing death was upon me. I arched my back, and with what little strength I had left, gave a final push. My fingers scrabbling at the lid one last time, I felt the tears fall from my eyes.

No more energy, nothing left, I lay spent, saw my fingers, nails all broken, skin ripped and bloody, didn't matter anymore. Nothing mattered anymore. No room to scream, no room to cry, no room to breathe . . . no air . . . no air . . . no air . . . one final thought: my wedding dress, all soiled now, and bloody too. My wedding ring, so bright, so new and shining on my finger . . . a bride, a bride, buried alive . . . no air . . . no air . . . no . . .

Blank . . . darkness . . . blackness, then light, then pain . . . more pain, and more. Why am I turning, why . . . wait . . . what now, what now? Strapped to a wheel, a wheel turning. Arms outstretched, and legs too. Wrists and ankles bound tight . . . can't move, I can't move. God help me. God help me. I am being flayed alive, flayed alive. Nothing in my head but pain, no memory of how or why. I am a strong man, tall and muscular, but reduced to pain, and all I am is pain.

Blank . . . darkness . . . blackness, then light . . . but no . . . but no, I want my mummy, I want my mummy. Screaming and crying, one thought and only one, I want my mummy. And I am not going without her, I can't. And you can't make me, I scream, and then I see, for just one moment, as I lie in the oxygen tent, just a little girl, a tunnel, a light, and a small boy, calling me. He wants to play with me, but I'm not going without my mummy, and he can't make me, no, he can't.

Watching, I see him turn away, I hear him say he's going to play anyway. Wait, wait, I want to go . . . and then the light . . . and then the light . . . and angels' wings . . . and lifting me . . . and lifting me . . . and angels' voices . . . calling me . . . they're calling me . . . and now I'm safe . . . and now I'm safe. . . .

Blank, darkness, blackness, then light, and I'm awake, and now I'm me.

Slowly I open my eyes. The first thing I do is look at my hands, my fingers. My nails are long, not broken and not bleeding, and relief floods over me.

"Are you okay?" I hear Mick ask, as he hands me a glass of water.

I nod, grateful for the water. "I'm back," I say, which leaves the question: Where then have I been?

The simple answer is, in trance, but who would be satisfied with that answer? Not I, not you the reader. I will attempt an explanation, even though, as I write, I wonder why I have begun this chapter at all . . . but my pen writes on, almost, it seems, without me.

In trance, a state in which I vacate my body so that those in the spirit world may use it, often to express who they are and how they died, I have experienced many lives. In this chapter I have briefly written of three of them. As I lived, or relived, those lives, I *was* that person, I felt, thought, heard, saw, and even smelled that person.

While I was in that trance state some of my friends, Mick McGuire, Adele Campion, and others, were with me, taping the session and witnessing my behavior. In each case I, or the subject, spoke my—their—thoughts, told my—their—story.

"I lay in the coffin, terrified, screaming, but hearing no sound, I recognized that the sound was in my head.

"Frantic, hardly able to breathe, I began to claw the lid. A futile act, but one I must perform, for I could not just be still and die, even knowing death was upon me. I arched my back, and with what little strength I had left, gave a final push. My fingers scrabbling at the lid one last time, I felt the tears fall from my eyes.

"...No room to scream...no room to breathe...no air... no air...no air...."

We were, my friends and I, engaged in what we believed to be rescue work. That is, we were helping those souls who feel the need to reenact their death experience in order to come to terms with it. The medium—I in this case—vacates her body and, with Grey Eagle watching and protecting, allows certain souls to use her body to express their needs.

Now the question for this chapter is: Were those lives my past lives? Was I in some kind of regressed state, recounting, reliving, my past lives? Or were these lives, these souls, separate from me, using my body to communicate, but otherwise unconnected to me?

There has been a great deal of work done in exploring reincarnation. Dr. Brian Weiss in his book *Many Lives, Many Masters* takes us on a fascinating journey of possibilities and explanations.

Of course, I have speculated upon the theory of other lives, past lives, and have wondered from time to time whether I was a princess or a lady-in-waiting or some glorious and romantic figure from another time. I smile as I write this, because although I don't mean to disparage the subject of reincarnation—indeed, as you will see, my thoughts are just the opposite—it amuses me when I hear people describe their past life experiences, and I question the authenticity of some. I can't help wondering why so few past life experiences are those of road sweepers or toilet cleaners, or others who led mundane and ordinary lives.

"Blank ... darkness ... blackness, then light, then pain ... more pain, and more. ... Strapped to a wheel ... arms outstretched, and legs too. Wrists and ankles bound tight ... can't move, I can't move. God help me. ... Nothing in my head but pain, no memory of how or why. I am a strong man, tall and muscular, but reduced to pain, and all I am is pain."

I remember once when I was in Hong Kong, an Australian man came to me for a consultation. I recall the session quite clearly as, for one thing, he was very tall, and had to bend to get through the door of my apartment. His session was a good one. We made contact with his family in the spirit world, and they were able to help him with his questions—that is, all but his last one. He asked, "So then, how many angels are with me right now?" And without waiting for my answer he said, "Six. At least six. They're with me all the time, you know."

I was speechless, but my client did not notice and went on, "I've had many lives, you know." This seeming confidence I knew he repeated to whoever would listen. "In fact, I was hoping you would give me healing. You see, I was a Roman centurion, oh, I don't remember how many lives ago, and during one of my battles I fell, and a whole army walked over me. My spine was crushed, and in every life I have had since then I have had to suffer severe back pain."

I looked at this man, well educated, in his late thirties, and shook my head in despair, knowing that what I had to say to him would fall on stony ground.

"I do have some advice," I said gently, and he leaned forward in eager anticipation. "As far as your angels go, I can't help, for I must be truthful and tell you I don't see any. But I can help with your back problem. Whether or not you were a Roman centurion and were crushed is immaterial to the back pain you are having now. The truth," I continued, "is that you are well over six feet tall, you have extremely bad posture, and you get virtually no exercise. Rectify these two things and I guarantee your back problem will be solved."

My client left, and I knew he would hold on to his belief, because in some strange way it gave comfort and meaning to his otherwise dull life.

But I digress. I seem to have moved away from my original question. Were the three experiences I had in trance my past lives or nothing to do with me personally at all?

"Blank...darkness...blackness, then light...but no...but no ...I want my mummy, I want my mummy. Screaming and crying, one thought and only one...just a little girl, a tunnel, a light, and a small boy, calling me...

"...and then the light...and then the light...and angels' wings...and lifting me...and lifting me...and angels' voices... calling me...they're calling me...and now I'm safe...and now I'm safe...."

It is my belief, based on many conversations with Grey Eagle, that the three experiences I have described and many others in my life were not at all to do with me, but were visits, visitors, from the spirit world, from souls who have needed my help. And if this can happen to me in a trance state, then I believe that it can happen to others in a regressed state or regression, a hypnotic state which is similar in many ways to a state of trance. So I guess what I am saying is that although a person may have an experience in trance or regression of another life, it would be wrong to assume that that life is somehow connected to the person, part of the person's past. It is possible for an entity in the spirit world, seeing an empty vehicle (for that is what a body in a trance state is), to seize the opportunity to use that body to connect with us on earth.

Now I know that this all sounds as if I am dismissing the theory of reincarnation, but I am not. And I think that rather than use my words to describe what I believe, I should tell you what I have learned from my teacher Grey Eagle.

First I must say that many people, in their attempt to explain reincarnation, refer to the mechanics by telling us that we live, we die, we go to the light, stay for a while, come back, live, die, go to the light, stay for a while, come back to earth, live, die, etc. I refer to it as the yo-yo syndrome.

Grey Eagle would say . . . we were, before we came to the earth world . . . we are, even as we live on earth . . . and we will continue to be after we have left this world. We are soul. As was the case before we came here to this earth, we had choices, and we chose this life. So when we die, we will have choices again. And before we make those choices we look to the needs of our soul, for it is the soul's growth that is the reason for our journeying. As we enter the light we may choose to stay still for a while, and most of us do, for in staying still we are able to become more centered, more knowing. At the right time—and that right time will be different for each of us—we will have the choice to move on. Some of us may choose to return to the earth plane, to be reincarnated in a physical body. Others, myself included (and with my limited knowledge, I say this knowing I may change my mind), may choose to explore the universe, and the many universes that are out there.

It is a frequent error to suppose that our world is the only one of any consequence even though we know that our earth is just a small speck of grit in relation to as much of the universe as we can see.

I am an explorer, I am inquisitive about people, which trait I know helps me in the work that I do. I am also a traveler, I enjoy new places and new experiences, so with my limited knowledge I will say that I would choose to travel the universe, explore the universe, rather than have another earth experience. But who knows? Only God, I suppose.

In the meantime, I do not concern myself with my past lives, if indeed I have any. I prefer instead to concentrate on the life I am leading now. To make this life the best that I can, and to try to learn my lessons here the best way I can. To enhance my soul's growth, to build my light, to be an example for the children of our earth. To have fun, to fill my life with laughter and with love.

Part II

LESSONS
AND INSIGHTS

"All these lessons, meant to teach us"

AND WE ARE SOUL. THIS TRUTH I KNOW, THIS TRUTH I ACCEPT. And, as I have just written in the last chapter, I believe each of us chose this life, that we made that choice prior to our birth here on this earth.

Each soul needs growth, needs enlightenment, and the reason we chose our life here is that this earth, this human existence, brings us many opportunities through our life experiences, allows us many lessons. Should we choose to believe that this is so—and I do—then again we face more choices. Do we acknowledge our lesson, acknowledge that each new day brings yet another new lesson? Do we take what is given and try to understand, to learn, to grow? Or do we close our eyes, walk blindly along our path, and, refusing to see life as our teacher, deny the soul its light, its growth, its enlightenment?

And we are soul. And each soul must make its choice, indeed, each day it *will* make its choice, for the way we choose to live each day is our decision.

I look back on some of my own life's experiences and I can see, in hindsight, many of my lessons. I recognize some truths, and discover some insights. Now, in this next section, by sharing with you a handful of these experiences, I perhaps can give you a little light, some insight into your own experiences, and perhaps you too may discover some truths.

Rape

It was 1986. We were on holiday with my boyfriend, Richard. It was the last vacation we would spend together.

There were two villas, joined, about three miles from the center of a little town on the island of Crete, one of the Greek islands in the Mediterranean. We had rented one of the villas for four weeks, and had rented a car, and the first week of the vacation had been good: the sun, the sea, good food, and plenty of rest, and Richard had been pleasant and easy. No black moods so far, no temperamental tantrums, which had become the pattern over the last eighteen months. Things looked good.

Richard had come into my life about two years after my husband had left. At first he had been all I could have wished a man to be—gentle, loving, kind. Samantha, then twelve years old, liked him too! He was good to her, as he was to me. Until the moods began.

When we first arrived at the villa we met our neighbors, who seemed to be nice people, but they stayed only for the first week. Then the trouble started. Four great hulking Welshmen moved in. Four great hulking, drinking, Rugby-playing Welshmen.

The first night they came home drunk and began shouting and

arguing loudly with one another. The walls of the villa were paper-thin. There was no way we couldn't listen, and the ruckus continued for a couple of hours.

The next morning they were outside on the deck having break-fast and Richard decided he should say something to them. "You were making a bit of a row last night, lads," he said good-naturedly, "and I don't want to spoil your fun, but could you keep the noise down a bit? We couldn't sleep."

"Sorry, mate," one of them replied. "Sure we will."

Once again in the early hours of the morning they rolled up drunk. Only this time they had a mission—to keep us awake. Banging on the wall, yelling obscenities, laughing at our discomfort, they made sure we didn't sleep for the next two hours.

For three nights the pattern remained the same, but the intensity grew. They argued and fought with one another, broke furniture and smashed windows. Finally, their threats against us getting louder and louder, they came onto our deck at the back of the villa and began beating on the windows, trying to break in.

Over those few days we hadn't been idle. We had contacted our travel agents and asked to be relocated. They refused. We had asked that our neighbors be removed. Again, our agents refused, and told us that everywhere was booked up. There was just nowhere else for either the Welshmen or us to go.

The people of the town knew the trouble we were having. They were having similar trouble, as the lads had been wrecking bars and picking fights with the locals. The owner of one of the hotels, sorry that he couldn't give us a room, did tell us that if we felt we were in serious danger we could go to his hotel, whatever time of day or night it was, and he would find us a bed.

Each night, as the violence and threats had increased, I watched and held my child as her terror grew. At sixteen she was a shy and somewhat timid girl. I had always been extremely protective of her, more so because her father had abandoned her, and watching her distress now was more than I could bear. I too, was afraid on that last night as we hurriedly packed an overnight bag and made a dash for the car and to safety, Samantha, terrified, sobbing in my arms.

We arrived at the hotel at around three in the morning, scared and shaking, and we were shown to a room. It took a while for me to settle Samantha. Eventually she fell asleep, but no matter how much I tried, sleep would not come to me. Instead I fought a battle. I was angry, perhaps more angry than I had ever been in my life, and in my mind I wanted to destroy those men for the harm they had caused my child. In my fury, I found myself imagining many dreadful things happening to them, and all I wanted was a terrible revenge.

However, Grey Eagle's teachings were strong, and I knew how wrong it was for me to feel this way. Our thoughts are our most powerful possession, and I was well aware that I could use my thoughts, turn them into a fearsome weapon, in the same way that I used my energy to create the wind in the story of Egypt, which was told in *The Eagle and the Rose*. I could project my energy, which in this case was anger, to do harm. I knew that if I were to concentrate all my thought energy on these men, the results would be devastating for them. And in the long hours of that night I wanted to harm them, I wanted to hit back. They had hurt my child.

But Grey Eagle's teachings are strong. First, he had taught me over the years that whatever thoughts I put out to the universe, positive or negative, I would receive back, tenfold. So to send out harmful and destructive thoughts would result in damaging myself—one very good reason not to take revenge. For me, though, a greater reason to control my thought energy was that I had learned over the years how important it was to exercise tolerance and create, wherever possible, peace and harmony. Only God and the universe could make true judgment.

So here I was, waging a war in my head between right action and wrong action, knowing that every action has its consequences, striving for right action, struggling to create a balance of peace and harmony within me, calling on God to help me find my light, and failing again and again.

Eventually morning came, and as we went down for breakfast my head was no clearer. I felt I had been battling with the devil within me, and I was still torn, knowing that my anger was wrong, harmful to me and to others, striving to combat and overcome it.

To anyone outside we would have seemed like any family on holiday. As we ate our breakfast, no one would have guessed our turmoil. But as I watched my child, quiet and reserved, my anger returned. It was the same for Richard. When we finished eating he suggested that Samantha and I stay at the hotel while he went back to the villa to fetch more things we might need for the next couple of days. He made this suggestion quietly, with no trace of anger or true intention in his voice, but I knew he meant to go back and confront these men.

"I'll go with you," I said. "Samantha can stay with the hotel staff for an hour. She'll be okay, and there are some things I want to collect."

Richard wouldn't hear of it, and it was only after some arguing and then my insistence that I would take a taxi and follow him that he finally gave in.

We arrived at the villa in silence. We noticed that one of the Welshmen had laid out a towel on the deck and was preparing for a spot of sunbathing. As soon as he saw us he retreated inside.

Up the steps of the villa we went. When I opened the door, Richard pushed me inside and slammed the door shut, thinking to lock me in. I knew where he was headed, and I knew there could be four rugby-playing louts ready and waiting to give him a beating.

Frantically I looked around the villa, searching for a weapon. My eyes fell on the beach umbrella stick we had bought just days before. It was about three feet long, sturdy and strong. I grabbed it and raced out the door. Richard's voice came to me from the back of the villa. I could hear him shouting for them to come out. "Come out and fight like men," he yelled. "No one threatens my family and gets away with it."

I headed around behind the two villas to where he stood, passing one of their bedroom windows. I looked in and saw the largest of them in bed, seemingly asleep. All the doors to their villa were open, and Richard was so angry now he didn't notice as I circled around him to the front. I looked through the front door. One of the men, tall and broad, stood just inside. He was facing Richard, and I could see straight through from one side of the room to the other, where the French windows were open and where Richard now stood, just outside. I could hear Richard yelling, "Get out here, all of you." But the man in the kitchen refused to move.

Clutching the hefty stick in my hands, I leaped into the kitchen, now the knight valiant, all thought of personal danger gone. "So," I heard myself say, my voice like ice, "he's too tough for you, is he? Then what about me? I'm just about your size, smaller than you, weaker than you, just how you all like it."

I lifted the stick in my hands, cold determination on my face, prepared to fight, prepared to fight them all. Then Richard, seeing the obvious danger I was in, stormed into the room. Quick as a flash, the man ran into the bedroom where I had seen his friend lying, banging the door hard behind him.

"Come on," said Richard. "Let's go. We've said our piece. There's no point hanging around."

But we hadn't said our piece, and it was not enough for me.

"No," I said, and clutching the umbrella stick tighter, I headed for the bedroom. The sight that met my eyes was pathetic. The man I had faced was lying on his bed, covered with suntan oil. In the next bed was the huge tub of lard, his back to me, pretending to be asleep.

As I lifted up the stick and brought it down with all my force on the bed where "sun oil" lay, I was calm, very calm. My words, as I spoke them, were said quietly, but yet with force. Again and again, first on one side of the bed, then the other, I brought the stick thudding down, as the man squirmed, crying now, every muscle in his body trembling with fright. The words I spoke were those of a mother defending her young, defending against rape. The fat tub of lard lay still in his bed, feigning sleep, until I took the stick and prodded him in the back. "And you," I said, "you with the yellow streak a mile wide down your back. What about you? I know you're awake, so what about you?"

Slowly he rolled over to face me and stared hard into my eyes. Unafraid, I stared back, telling him that he would remember me for the rest of his bullying, miserable life, for he would never, ever, forget that a woman had faced him down. His eyes fell, and he turned his back on me once again.

I turned my attention back to the other one, and again I brought down the stick with as much force as I could muster, telling him that no one could scare my child and get away with it, that he, too, would live the rest of his life remembering me, that never again would he bully anyone without seeing my face and knowing what he was.

As I brought the stick down for the final time I heard Grey Eagle's voice, calm and gentle, in my ear: "You may do this, child, but do not touch him, do not harm him, for you will only harm yourself."

A few days later, all four men were taken by the Greek police and evicted from the island. Two each had a broken arm, one a broken collarbone. All were bruised and battered. The local boys had had enough and had given them all a good beating.

I couldn't help thinking that for once, perhaps justice had been done.

And I heard Grey Eagle's voice, calm and gentle, in my ear: "You may do this, child, but do not touch him, do not harm him, for you will only harm yourself."

Ordinarily, when the word "rape" is mentioned, we automatically think of physical rape—the rape of a child, the rape of a woman, which is a most terrifying and damaging experience, and which cannot be compared to any other act, for in this act there occurs a terrible violation not only of the body, but of the mind and spirit also. But the raping of the mind, which occurs frequently with so many of us, is not to be ignored or made less of for the lack of physical abuse. And the perpetrators of this act, not violent criminals but often ordinary and generally nice people, would no doubt throw up their hands in horror at the very idea that they could be termed rapists.

But rapists they are, for any act which is designed to rob someone of self-worth, self-esteem, and confidence is an act of rape. And in this type of rape there are many willing victims—people who already have little self-esteem, who do not value themselves, who feel that they deserve no better.

For many years I was a willing victim, having been brought up to believe that I was of no consequence. I had no idea what valuing oneself meant, and I allowed myself as an adult to be abused. That is, I stood still and did nothing to prevent abuse. Like many, after my divorce, telling myself that I would never let anyone treat me badly again, I walked straight into another abusive relationship. I was never beaten physically, but emotionally I was black and blue, trying yet again to make the square peg fit into the round hole, desperate not to fail again, and all the time, without realizing it, failing myself.

Richard was a good man; in many ways he was loving and kind. Our relationship would not have lasted seven years but for this, and for my determination to succeed. I desperately did not want to fail. But his black moods became worse and worse. He was a Jekyll and Hyde; he had a dual personality. One moment he could be the nicest and most loving man. The next moment, and for no apparent reason, he would become an ogre, and eventually I reached my breaking point.

This was to be the last time in my life that I stood still and allowed myself to be the victim. In some ways it was the worst situation I had been in since my childhood, but in one way it was the best.

It was perhaps ten days after the incident with the Welshmen. We had finally been able to move, had found a villa up in the mountains, and having become friendly with the Greek family who owned the villa, we were invited by them to a barbecue. It was a holy day celebration and the entire village turned out. Whole lambs were roasted, wonderful Greek salads and good breads were laid out on trestle tables. The festivities were held among the olive groves.

When we were first invited to the party I had felt I would have to refuse. I had for the last six months suffered great discomfort with my periods. My menstrual cycle was shot to pieces and I had been bleeding heavily for weeks and weeks. It was so bad there were times I would hardly dare stand up if I had been sitting down even for a few moments for fear of flooding. On a few occasions I had driven somewhere only to find I couldn't get out of the car because I was such a mess. So going to a party in an olive grove (no ladies' room, no toilet facilities) seemed out of the question.

However, Richard suggested that it would be possible. "I'll just bring you back here," he said. "We can come back as often as you like, and then you won't need to worry."

Doubtfully, knowing how easily his mood changed, I made him promise that there would be no fuss, and he agreed.

The night air was warm and sweetly scented, as only the air on a Greek island can be. Beautiful olive-skinned girls and handsome dark-eyed men danced and sang. The older women watched, laughing at their husbands dancing with the young ones, clapping in time to the music. And I laughed and sang, and watched as

58

Samantha danced with the younger girls, happy that we were having such a good time.

After an hour or so, Richard suggested we go back to the villa so that I could freshen up. Grateful for his suggestion and his good humor, I nodded my agreement, and after checking that Samantha was okay we headed for the car. The villa was only five minutes' drive away.

We had parked inside the olive grove by the side of a ditch, and so Richard made his way out to the road. It was as we waited for the traffic to ease so that we could make a right turn that Richard's mood changed.

"Bloody f'ing traffic," he suddenly yelled. "Do they think I've got all bloody night?" With that he yanked the steering wheel to the left.

At that moment I knew I was in trouble. I begged and pleaded with him to turn the car around to go back to the villa, but he didn't answer me, just kept on cursing. Then, maybe three miles on, he pulled the car to the side of the road and switched off the engine.

"Here," he said, "you can do it here." I looked at him in horror, knowing that he meant it. It was true that I had tampons and sanitary towels and tissues in the car. Because of my condition it had been necessary to carry them. But I couldn't believe what I was hearing.

Choking back my tears, I tried again, pleading with him to take me back to the villa. "I can't change here," I sobbed. "This is a busy road. Please, Richard, just take me home."

To my relief he started the car, but my relief was short-lived, as he just drove a short way down the road to a pulloff area. He pulled in and switched off the engine, and as he got out of the car he growled. "This is it, I'm not f'ing moving again, so just climb in the back and get on with it."

There were other cars in the pulloff, and as I crouched down in my seat, I didn't know if they could see me or not. Afraid to switch on the interior light and knowing I had no choice but to do what Richard said, I took off my pants and my panties and began to clean myself up, groping in the dark, not knowing what condition I was in, feeling bloody and sticky.

From time to time Richard would stick his head in the window, cursing and swearing, calling me a bitch and worse, telling me to get a move on. At one point I screamed at him. I can hear that scream now as I write. I hated him for defiling me, and I hated myself more for the cringing filthy thing I felt I was.

Soon it was over and I climbed back into the front seat of the car. I didn't know how I looked, if my pants were stained or if my hands were bloody. I needed to wash, but not just to wash my hands. I felt the need to scrub and scrub my body, to clean myself all over.

We drove back to the olive grove in silence. It was only when we had parked the car and began walking toward where our friends sat that Richard came to life. Grabbing my hand, desperation in his voice, he begged me to forgive him. "I know I've done it this time, I've gone too far," and on and on. But I was too numb to respond. My only thought now was that I must not spoil this evening for my friends or for my daughter. And, as all of us do in these situations, I put on a good face and no one guessed.

It was time for the last dance, and all but the old and infirm joined in. Richard reached for me, and I knew I could not refuse, for if I did, Samantha would see straight through my act. His arms encircled me, and he drew me close to him in a loving embrace, whispering that he was sorry and that he loved me. The air was warm and sweet-scented, a night for romance, a night for love. I no longer felt hate, for the hate that I had felt for him and for myself was too powerful, too all-consuming, and would have burned me out.

I felt his arms tighten about me, felt his lips in my hair . . . and then pictures flashed through my mind. I heard my ex-husband's voice, saw myself naked stepping out of the bath, saw myself cringing, trying to cover up my body as his eyes roamed over me. I could hear his words, see the sneer on his face: "There is nothing," he said, "*nothing*, that I find attractive about you."

Another picture. I was almost fifteen. It was morning, I was in my pajamas, jacket buttons open, wearing an undershirt. I had taken a cup of tea in to my mother, and thinking she was asleep, I was about to leave. She grunted and motioned me closer to the bed. Then, so fast, her hand shot out and grabbed my undershirt. She yanked it up, her face twisted with contempt as she looked at my still-undeveloped chest. She snorted, let go of my undershirt, and motioned me out of the room. I fled, shame and humiliation burning through me.

These things I saw as Richard held me.

Another picture. Now I am small, perhaps only four or five years old. When I sleep I tuck my hands between my legs, and as all little girls do, although I didn't know it then, I would play with myself. I wake up, feel the dread, know that my father is home. I see myself, so small, so small, standing with bowed head. I hear my father's voice: "Lift up your hands, let me smell your fingers." I know he will smell me, I know he will beat me because I am so dirty...they tell me so...they tell me so...they must be right...they tell me so.

I feel his arms about me, so tender, so loving, as I stand in the olive grove, and great loneliness fills my soul. Then the resolution—I will not be raped again...I will never accept rape passively again.

When we arrived back in England I ended my relationship with Richard and began my relationship with myself.

Sounds easy. Reads easy. Why is it so hard to do? Because we have to get rid of the old stuff. Because we have to look at ourselves. And we have to be honest.

The truth is that we have all, at some stage in our lives, been the victim, willing or not.

A worse truth, and one we have to face if we really want a good relationship with our own self, is that we have all, at some point or another in our lives, been the rapist. This is hard to face, and most of us would initially deny this fact. But fact it is. When we are angry we lash out, we hurt, we "take away." Sometimes we make a joke . . . at someone else's expense, we "take away."

In my life I have done and said many things in anger, or out of frustration. I am not guiltless. I am basically a nice person, but my behavior over the years has not been irreproachable. My record is not unblemished. I have lashed out, with no good reason, although at those times I have probably given myself any number of excuses. When two people are in fierce argument, depending on your point of view, both could be seen to be the victim or to be the rapist, for each is "taking away" from the other. Each is allowing someone to "take," and each is "taking from."

As with any belief system, whether it be religion, politics, child-rearing, or business, no one person is always right or always wrong. To force one's own beliefs upon others is to try to rob them of what they believe is right. Notice that I use the word "force." The definition of the word "rape," according to *Webster's Dictionary*, is "an act or instance of robbing or despoiling a person by force."

Having finally reached the point in my life when my relationship with myself became more important than my relationship with others, I knew I had to take a good hard look at myself. I needed to discover who and what I had allowed myself to become.

Facing one's self is not an easy task, and it would have been easy for me to beat myself over the head with a hard and heavy stick. But Grey Eagle has taught me to be gentle with myself, and so this undertaking was not as difficult as it might have been. There were, I discovered, many events in my life that I was ashamed to have been a participant in—nothing truly wicked, but many things to reproach myself for, many acts that I must confess embarrassed and shamed me, for I had been the perpetrator of these acts, the rapist. But one act stands out in my mind perhaps more than any other.

It was many years ago, almost thirty. I was not quite twenty-one. I had been very sick and could easily have died. My surgeon told me that I had been born with a kidney defect, that I had always, unknowingly, been sick.

A few weeks after I was eventually allowed out of the hospital, my then-husband and I visited my parents, at their home, where my sisters were also visiting. I remember we had eaten lunch, and perhaps it was that I was sick, but a rare feeling of camaraderie settled among us and we pulled our chairs to the fire and began to talk. My father, in the rarest mood, and somewhat compassionately, began to talk about my illness. His guilt about the kind of father he had been showed, although he never acknowledged it, as he spoke a little about my childhood and the fact that I must have experienced pain or discomfort in my back and kidneys and that no one had been aware of it.

I was sitting opposite him, but close, and without thought I uttered the words I would regret for the rest of my life. "Yes," I said, "and just think of all the beatings you gave me, and all the time I was so sick."

I had been looking directly at him as I said those words, and if I had stabbed him in the heart with a sharp knife the effect would not have been worse. He flinched visibly, and his face paled with shock. But it was the look I saw in his eyes that I will never forget. I had cut him to the heart, and as he bled I saw his pain, great pain from the hurt that I had caused.

I have told this story a few times, and each time I tell it, especially to people who have read my first book, the response is the same. "You had every right." "Look what he did to you." "He deserved it." And so on. But I must be honest. When I spoke those words and saw my father's reaction I was ashamed. I felt a deep sense of shame for what I had done, for I knew that my father was at that moment vulnerable. He was trying in his own way to say he was sorry, and in that moment, when he was reaching out to me, I took away from him. And that made me no better than he when, as a child and vulnerable, he took away from me.

No amount of self-justification will convince me that I was not wrong. I sensed an opportunity to kick someone when he was down. I knew I was worthy of more than that, better than that. My soul is a gentle soul, and I denied my father, and therefore I denied myself the necessary gentleness that enhances and gives light to the soul.

I cannot take away the deed, nor erase the words. I cannot ease my father's pain, the pain of that moment, the pain that I caused. I can only say that, having lacked compassion, I must strive to be more compassionate. For as much as I refuse to be a willing victim, I must surely guard against being a rapist.

We Don't
Like You Anymore

Throughout the last chapter it is fairly obvious that one of the lessons we can learn is that to cause harm to another is to cause harm to your own self. In this next chapter I try to show how easy it is, through negative action and negative thought, to cause harm, not just to others here on the earth plane, but to those in the spirit world too.

It was Friday night, class night in my healing organization, and there were about a dozen students, plus the teacher—me. As usual I hadn't planned ahead, hadn't strategized. I knew I would be guided, that Grey Eagle would guide me, and as we sat, my students and I, my senses, always acute, told me we had visitors.

At first I heard them as they moved silently into the room, whispering to one another. Then I saw them one by one, until they were a small group huddled together. Children, about twenty of them, their ages ranging from four years to perhaps ten or eleven. One, a boy of about seven, stepped forward. He would be the spokesman, and, I suspected, our teacher for the evening.

He gave me no name, nor throughout the evening did any of the others. It was unimportant, it seemed, for them to tell us who they were. It was only important that we listen to what they had to say.

I told my students what was happening, then we waited. I knew the children would tell us when they were ready to begin.

The boy came closer. I could feel his energy, and instinctively I knew the way he wanted to communicate. In similar circumstances I have often gone into a trance state, allowing the person in the spirit world to use my body, my voice box, and this way of expression will often bring startling results, as this form of coalescing, of union, dispels all barriers.

The boy came closer still, but we were not to communicate in trance, but in a way which I can only describe to you as a union of minds, more than telepathy, for every thought and every feeling is exchanged. I became almost, but not quite, the boy, and as his words fill my mind I become so relaxed and so joined to him that his words spill out of my mouth with no effort and no resistance on my part at all. My body becames so still, all movement is slowed, and an inexperienced observer might think that I am asleep. But my mind is sharp, and I am finely attuned as this boy and I fuse together, and now, the link complete, his words begin to tumble from my mouth, and our lesson begins.

"You were cleaning, we saw you, outside, in the outhouse. A mop and bucket of soapy water, and you were scrubbing."

This, a statement, not a question, the boy had directed at one of our students, Pat Mason. She looked confused, but nodded, wondering where this was going.

"The girls came, Jenny and Helen," continued the boy, referring to Pat's teenage daughters. "They only wanted to talk to you. You screamed at them, you yelled at them to go away. You didn't want to scrub and clean. You were in a bad mood, and you were mean. We saw you, we were watching, and the girls . . . and we don't like you anymore."

As he said this, the group of children came a little closer to him, nodding their agreement. They all felt the same.

Pat, startled, hung her head. A tear ran down her face. She sat in shamed silence.

Then, without waiting, the boy moved on to Betty, another student.

"You were decorating the bedroom. We watched you with your husband. He is a nice man. You were both working hard. You sat on the floor. It wouldn't go right, and you got mad and yelled at him, blamed him when he wasn't wrong. And you were mean to him. We saw you, we were watching, and your husband . . . and we don't like you anymore."

Betty, who at some point during this exchange had gasped and held her hand to her mouth, now nodded as she remembered what she had done. The realization that she had been seen and heard was a shock to her.

And then to Joan, recounting how they had seen her, grumbling and groaning over some small incident. Again he said, "We saw you, you were mean . . . and we don't like you anymore."

For the next forty minutes each student received his or her message from the boy. And although each student's reaction was different, they all felt shame. Peter Boulton, the chairman of our healing organization, the Rosemary Altea Association of Healers, was a student there that night also. Along with the rest of the class, he too was made by these children in the spirit world to face the fact that at some point over the previous week he had acted badly, even meanly and thoughtlessly, toward someone he loved.

And over and over, as the evening progressed, we heard the boy. "We saw you, we were watching you, and them, and you were mean . . . and we don't like you anymore."

As the last student was given this message I looked to the children. Now all had drawn close to me, and all were nodding. Their expressions were cheerless, and I sensed from them some disappointment and sadness.

There was just one more student left, and I looked at the boy, at the children, and asked, "So what of me? What do you have to say to me?"

The boy smiled, for the first time, and the children smiled with him. "Not for you," he said. "This lesson is not for you. For you are one who sees us, who knows that we are there. And when you shout, and when you yell, and when you are mean, you see us watching, and you know. We see you, we watch you, and we hear you say...I don't like me anymore."

The room is silent, each student struggling with this lesson, feeling shame, hurting with the pain of being discovered, pain in discovering these children's pain. Not one of us will say "I am sorry," for each of us knows that "sorry" is just a word.

Yet through our pain, and through our shame, each one of us is grateful. For even though the lesson is a hard one, we strive to learn, and are thankful for our teachings, no matter what form they take. And more, we are filled with gratitude for our teachers, those in the spirit world who care enough to shine a light on human conduct.

Now, having read this story, you must understand that all of these students are healers, or potential healers—people who are on a spiritual path, who have asked to be taught, who know, or at least strive to know, the great responsibility a healer has. Therefore the lessons they receive may be harsh ones, or seem to be.

Had I sat with them and discussed the fact that those in the spirit world watch us, and are affected by our actions, without their first having experienced these children, who are saddened by our behavior, my students would not have been so moved. How much better the lesson, how much greater the impact, when the teaching is given this way, in a way my students certainly will never forget.

We are of the universe. The universe is of us. Unseparate, inseparable, one. Our actions create reactions. And each of us, each individual, is responsible for those actions.

68

We are not, I believe, required by God to be superhuman. The universe understands and accepts our human faults and failings. If we are mean sometimes, angry sometimes, flustered, confused, and aggressive sometimes, then those who are of the universe will look on us with sad eyes, but with great compassion and understanding for our human frailties. But also we must know, and we must remember, that in these times the universe will shake a little, and become darker, for we are of the universe. When we perform an act of mean-spiritedness, then our light, our spirit, becomes dimmed, and the universe, and our soul, loses a little of that light.

The reverse, however, is also true. When we commit an act of kindness, of gentleness, an act of joy, then our light, our spirit self, becomes brighter, shines like a beacon out into the universe, and the universe trembles, and absorbs that light joyfully, and becomes brighter.

The children of the spirit world who came to us that night came because they cared. They were chosen by Grey Eagle. They volunteered not because they really didn't like us, not because they wanted to hurt and shame us. That was never their intention. But when a caring teacher needs to impart very necessary knowledge to his or her students, when time is limited and the lesson needs to be learned well, then the teacher will ask, "How can I achieve the greatest impact?" And the answer, in this case, and for these students, was "Out of the mouths of children." From a child's eyes they perhaps will see more clearly.

It worked, for not one student was left unmoved. Not one student refused the lesson. And not one student omitted to thank the children and show gratitude for the gift of a child's insight. Oh, how a child can teach us, if we, the adults, will only listen.

I would like to end this chapter not with my words but with the words of Pat Mason, one of the students there that night. She says:

Like the others in the class, I was a little stunned to discover these truths about myself, but accepting the lesson and trying to apply it to my everyday life has helped me in my resolve to maintain a positive and joyful outlook, whatever unpleasantness I have to face.

In dealing with any situation, knowing I am in the presence of trusting and impressionable children obliges me to remain calm and rational, clear in my thinking, and realistic in my expectations of myself and others. It also helps to curb any inclination toward self-indulgent grumbling and self-pity.

I feel I have a three-year-old holding my hand, albeit a child in the spirit world, and I have a joyful obligation to notice and share with him or her all the things that have ever brought me happiness, to help make his or her world as beautiful as I can. As a result, looking for old and new joys to experience has left no space in my life for anxiety and self-doubt, and these two almost constant companions of the past are well on their way to oblivion.

As always, the child leads and teaches the adult.

And a poem:

> *One night he heard you singing*
> *Of love and hope and joy*
> *Drew near to see if you could want*
> *Another little boy*
>
> *He wants to comfort you in times of fear*
> *And to soothe your pain*
> *But you cannot take his comfort*
> *For you never knew he came*
>
> *You never knew, when angry*
> *When your voice was shrill to hear*
> *With your fury and frustration*
> *That a little child stood near*
>
> *Make no mistake, you drove him out*
> *His love you did deny*

LESSONS AND INSIGHTS

Too full of selfish pitying
Yet still he is nearby

Why don't you see the joy you miss
He comes to show to you
Through you he looks out on the world
Should he be bitter too?

He needs to give his love to you
As much as you to him
So find yourself, and find your joy
And welcome him back in

Now every time you feel your pain
Each time you shed a tear
Don't miss what really matters
For a little child stands near

PATRICIA MASON
Healer member, RAAH

My Own
Small Miracles

Does it happen to me?

This is a question so often asked that I thought it would be good to talk just a little about it directly.

So many people think that because my life is so blessed, because I have such a special gift, how could I personally have any problems in my own life? I have heard people say, "Doesn't Grey Eagle give you all the answers? Doesn't he smooth away all the wrinkles?" The straight answer is no, he does not.

I have said so often that pain and conflict are our teachers, along with joy and excitement. Happiness and fear frequently go hand in hand. They are emotions, felt through experience, and emotion is our educator.

How could I learn, how could I grow, without a variety of experiences, pleasant and unpleasant? How could I explore myself through my emotions if those emotions were only ones that gave me pleasure? It would be like going to school and studying only my favorite subjects. No more math, no more science, no more hard work struggling to understand things that don't interest me, even though common sense tells me that the subjects I dislike are still necessary, still of use to me in my daily life. So, of course, if all the hard stuff were taken away from me, my growth process would be inhibited. That means I have problems, just like everyone else. I have the same concerns about health, relationships, children, business, money, home—all the concerns of a normal person, which is what I consider myself to be.

However, I am fortunate enough to know some things that others don't. And I am blessed with Grey Eagle, who far from giving me all the answers to my many, many, questions, indeed shows me how to explore my own mind and the knowledge with which I was born. Through him I have learned one very valuable lesson—that there is not one question we can ask that some-where, deep within the recesses of the soul, we do not have the answer to.

I believe too that each of us, in any given situation in our lives, has a helper, a friend or relative in the spirit world, or an angel, who will stand close by us in our times of need, ready to steer and direct us, if only we knew how to listen. But this subject is for another time, another book.

I could give you many examples of how I personally have been helped by Grey Eagle and the spirit world, but time and space are short, so here are just a few.

At the very beginning, when I first discovered my gift of mediumship, after meeting Paul Denham and Mick McGuire, I had begun to recognize and to trust the hand of God and the spirit world. Sometimes in the littlest ways, I began to comprehend the wisdom, insight, and capability of the power of the universe.

A SMALL THING

I was in the post office, in a long line of people who, like me, were there to collect their state benefit. I hated it, hated being poor, hated the undignified and humiliating lineup, but like many others there, I had no choice. My husband had long since gone with his new girlfriend. He had taken all the money and left Samantha, then aged ten, and me to starve. So for the first time in my life I had applied for, and received, a small state benefit—equivalent to thirty-five U.S. dollars a week. With that I had to feed and clothe us and pay the mortgage and the bills. It was impossible, and many of the bills, of course, went unpaid.

One of those, the electricity bill, had been handed to me by the postman as I'd walked up the drive on my way into the village. I had torn open the envelope with dread, knowing that no matter how small the amount, I would not be able to pay it. It was a red bill, overdue. Pay *immediately* or be cut off, I read. The amount was just under twenty-two pounds, nearly the entire benefit amount. I bit my lip, more pressure mounting, and determined not to cry, I shoved the bill back into its envelope and stuffed it in my purse.

The line inched forward. There were now only five people in front of me, and I reached into my purse and pulled out my state benefit book. Inadvertently, out came the electricity bill too, and I hastily pushed it back in.

Then I heard the voice: "Pay the bill," it said.

Of course this was a joke, a voice to be ignored. I looked to the front of the line, wondering how much longer I would have to stand here.

The line moved forward again. Now there were only three people ahead of me. The wait seemed interminable.

Another movement, now only two ahead. Then the voice again, a man's voice, much stronger now: "Pay the bill, pay the electricity bill."

I shook my head, trying to shake the voice away. It was the most ridiculous thing I had ever heard. One, I had no money in my wallet, not a penny. Two, the money from my benefit was to buy food for my child. Not only was my wallet empty, my food cupboards were empty also. Three, who was this man anyway? Who was he to tell me what to do? I knew my priorities, and now my priority was food.

More movement. Now just one person ahead of me. Thank God, I thought, my humiliation growing by the second.

Now my turn, and I stepped up to the counter and pushed my book through the window.

"Pay the bill, pay the bill." The voice was now so much more a command than a request that I reached into my bag, pulled out the bill, and handed it over the counter. As the clerk snatched it up, I heard myself meekly say, "And I would like to pay the bill, please."

Wide-eyed, I watched her take the bill from the envelope, pull some money from a drawer and count it out, and stamp the bill "paid." Speechless, unable to stop the process, I stood at the counter and waited for my change. Coppers, coppers, that's all there were. The clerk pushed them over the counter toward me, a bright smile on her face.

The lump in my throat threatened to choke me as I raced to the door. In my haste, I practically fell into the street, the coppers clutched tightly in my hand.

Once outside, standing alone and so lonely in the summer sun, I opened my hand and gazed down in dismay at the pennies there. "Oh God," I thought, "what am I going to do, what am I going to do?" There was no food in the house, not much milk, nothing for Samantha's dinner. As I write this it is hard for me to believe that we were so poor and so desperate all those years ago, but I remember how I walked home. The walk that day seemed endless, even though it took just twenty minutes, and I cried all the way home, unaware if anyone noticed me. I trudged up the hill, tears running down my cheeks, and I scolded myself over and over for being so stupid, so very, very stupid.

I arrived home and immediately went into the kitchen to put on the kettle. I drank tea in those days. I found that if I drank a lot of tea I wouldn't get so hungry. Taking my tea through into the living room, I sank down into a chair and, still crying, tried to figure out what I could give Samantha to eat when she came home from school. There was little choice, just toast and margarine. I couldn't stop crying.

Thirty minutes passed while I sat huddled in the chair. Then a knock came at the door. I wasn't expecting anyone, but debt collectors never warned of their arrival, and there had been many of those over the last few months. This time, though, I didn't care, didn't hide as I'd often done. When my visitor rapped on the door again, I wearily got up to answer it.

The young couple who stood there could have been no more than twenty. He was tall and fair-haired, and very handsome. She, small, dark, and pretty, made a good contrast to his blond looks. They were not what I expected to see, and for a moment I was confused and speechless.

"We've been sent by the owner of the hardware store," stammered the young man, who had obviously taken my silence as disapproval. "She said you might rent us a room. We've tried everywhere else with no luck, and we're desperate."

Still I stood, not uttering a word. Now I was speechless for another reason. A room? To rent? What did they mean? What were they talking about? I didn't rent rooms out. Finally I found my voice and expressed this fact to them. Then the girl spoke.

"My mother kicked us out," she said, and started to cry. "And he," looking at the young man, "he has a job on an oil rig near here, and we can't find anywhere to stay. The lady at the store said you might help. Please," she added, "we have nowhere else to go."

She was obviously distressed, they both were. "You had better come inside," I said gently. "I'm not sure I can help, but I can listen."

In they came, and I can picture them now, a desperate young

couple, in love and homeless. They sat on the sofa and told me their story, not an unusual one. Fights with Mum, misunderstandings. And they had walked out.

"If you let us have a room," the boy said, "it will only be for a couple of weeks, four at the most, and we won't be any trouble, I promise."

"But I don't take boarders," I replied. "I wouldn't know how to begin. I really don't know what to say."

"Well," he said, "we would pay you the going rate, and I'd be happy to give you two weeks in advance." With that he pulled some notes out of his wallet. "Forty pounds a week, two weeks, that's eighty pounds. If that isn't acceptable, let me know. We'll provide our own food. This money is just for the room. Okay?"

For the third time in less than an hour I was speechless. All I could do was nod my head.

The girl started to cry again, relieved now. Her boyfriend put his arm around her and lifted her up off the sofa, giving her a big hug. "We'll go fetch our stuff," he said, and noticing the startled look on my face, he smiled and said, "Don't worry—it's just a couple of small bags. We're traveling light." And with that they were gone, leaving me to stare at the money he had put into my hand. No need to worry about feeding my child tonight!

They stayed for six months, until he was transferred to another location. I remember them and smile, for they were lovely—pleasant, and fun, and in love. I hope that wherever they are, together or separate, they are happy.

I look back on that time and I remember the voice: "Pay the bill, pay the bill." Such a little amount. It seems impossible now to think that just twenty-two pounds, or the lack of it, could have broken me.

But I heard the voice. I almost ignored it, and I thank God that I didn't. It was a great lesson to me, and it taught me to trust.

At the time, that electricity bill was the straw that almost broke the camel's back. Such a big deal, yet really...just a small thing. One small miracle.

TRULY UNBELIEVABLE

It was December, and we were in for a white Christmas. Storms and blizzards raged, and the whole country was slowly coming to a standstill. The weathermen warned, "Don't go out unless you really have to." Several weeks earlier I had arranged to meet Andrew, as usual, a few days before Christmas. Only since my first love when I was sixteen—his name was John—had I loved as I loved Andrew. He was a Scotsman, and we lived far apart from each other. For many reasons a full-time relationship was impossible, but over the years, although we hardly saw each other and led separate lives, we loved each other dearly.

Christmas was that one time in the year when we made a special effort to meet, but this year was proving difficult. Tuesday came around, and the weather was worsening. Anxiously I followed the forecasts, hoping that tomorrow would be better. But Tuesday evening I was facing a dilemma. Should I go or shouldn't I? Would the roads be passable? And the big question—would the car survive the journey?

My car was old and battered and very temperamental, and it would often break down. Although I had never actually been stranded, I had to consider that there could be a first time. What should I do? Andrew was unreachable, because he was traveling. In those days no one carried a cell phone or had a fax machine.

I asked the question: Did I want to go? The answer...definitely yes. Next question: Did I want to risk life and limb? Definitely no. It was at this point, unable to think rationally anymore, that I looked to my guide. He smiled his gentle smile, and softly touching my cheek, he said, "If you must go, then we will keep you safe. Don't worry, child, you will make it there, and you will make it back. We will protect you and you will remain safe." That was enough for me, as I trusted Grey Eagle implicitly. And so early on Wednesday morning I set off to the meeting place.

For the first twenty miles I had to use country roads, which had not been cleared by snowplows, and driving was difficult, but not impossible. However, I had gone only about twelve miles when I began to doubt the sanity of my journey, and was at the point of asking Grey Eagle once again if I would be okay when it happened.

There were no other cars on the road. The fields I passed by were covered with snow, and although the snow had been falling hard and steadily throughout the night, there were only flurries now as I wound my way through the deserted villages toward the main highway. Then there was a loud bang, like the sound of an exploding cannon, and a flash of light, bright purple, lit the sky to my left. I turned to look, for a moment blinded and somewhat startled, my hands instinctively gripping the steering wheel hard. The light, there in an instant, was as quickly gone, with nothing to show that it had been there at all. I turned my attention back to the road . . . and saw the unbelievable.

There have been many times throughout my life when I have seriously doubted my sanity. I have seen and experienced much that was beyond my comprehension, beyond belief. As I write this story I can offer you, the reader, no proof my words are true. I can only tell you what I saw.

Sitting cross-legged, his back to me, perched a small boy, or so at first I thought. Judging by his size, I guessed he was about five years old. He was dressed in dark pants, a white shirt with bil-lowed sleeves, Eastern-style, and a conical hat, wide-brimmed at the base, which had a long piece of white muslin, pinned to one side, fastened under his chin, the rest, caught by the wind, flying over his shoulder.

I was taken completely by surprise, my eyes widened, my mouth fell open, and it took a few moments before I could recover sufficiently to ask him who he was. It was on hearing the words— not spoken out loud, but "voiced" in the way I often speak with those in the spirit world, with my mind—that he turned his head, looking at me over his shoulder, grinning at my surprise. I realized then he was not a child but a man. His eyes twinkled, and with one hand he stroked his goatee beard as he answered me. "I am sent to take care of the car," he said. "To make sure that your journey is a safe one, and that you return home without difficulty." This last was said in such a matter-of-fact way that I was in no doubt he not only meant what he said, but would do what he said.

I looked to Grey Eagle, not understanding the need for anyone other than him to steer my path, but was instantly reassured by his words. "Trust, child, we know what is needed here, and there is no need for further questions." And so, quite simply, I accepted.

The highway was a nightmare. Three lanes, but two of them closed, the third just passable, and driving was slow. Finally I reached my exit, but as I reached the top of the incline the engine cut out. I gazed in horror at the dials which were registering zero, and had no option but to coast down the hill.

"But, but..." I moaned, panic for one moment reaching my brain. Then I saw the garage at the bottom of the hill and steered the car into it.

It was a small problem, easily fixed. "But only temporary," said the mechanic. "Make sure you get it fixed properly as soon as you can."

Andrew and I had lunch together, swapped news, and celebrated our own small Christmas, and by midafternoon I was on my way home, praying that the car would hold out.

The journey back was endless, three hours, no heating now, as whatever the problem was had disabled the heater. So I froze, and I prayed, and I froze and I prayed.

Twenty miles from home, relieved that I was on the final stretch, but concerned now, as the snow was falling heavily, I stopped at a traffic light, intending to drive straight on.

"Turn right here," I heard Grey Eagle say.

"But that's not the right way," I replied.

"The road ahead is blocked," Grey Eagle returned, "but don't worry, we'll use the roads that have been cleared."

From that point I followed Grey Eagle's instructions—turn left, go right, slow down here, there's ice, and so on. The car was now choking and spluttering from time to time, making my heart miss a beat, fearing that it would just stop dead.

Finally I turned the corner into my own street, the car bucking a little as I did so, and as I steered the car into the driveway it cut out completely and rolled to a stop in front of the garage. Grey Eagle's words rang in my ears: "You will make it there, and you will make it back. We will protect you, and you will remain safe."

When I recounted this story to my friends later, I remember shaking my head, saying, "Unbelievable—it was simply *unbelievable.*"

Perhaps two or three years later, I was high in the sky, flying to some country or other, I don't remember which. I was reading a book, and there was nothing special on my mind. For no reason at all, I felt compelled to look out the window, to turn and look at the wing of the plane behind me. Imagine my delight, then concern, then pleasure, when I saw the little man, sitting cross-legged on the wing, somewhat like a genie on a magic carpet, his long scarf, pinned under his chin, floating high above his shoulder. He grinned at me, and I grinned back, then, turning, I mused a moment before continuing with my book. "Perhaps we have engine trouble, or some small mechanical fault," I thought. "Well, whatever it is, I know we'll all be safe." I took a moment more, looking around at the other passengers on the plane, wondering what their reactions would be if they knew, if they too could see my friend out there on the wing. Reaching for my book, taking one more look over my shoulder, taking time to wave and say thank you, I smiled, knowing that my fellow passengers would simply not believe their eyes. And if I were to tell them that the little man on the wing was real, I knew without a doubt that my story, like an Arabian fairy tale, would be impossible to believe, quite simply . . . *unbelievable*. And yes . . . another small miracle.

LITTLE THINGS

When I look back on my life, there have been so many times when all seemed lost, and without warning some small thing would happen and help in one form or another arrived. Sometimes the experience was stunning, as in the last story. At other times it was the smallest thing. But miracles don't always come with a big bang, and God bestows his miracles, I believe, often in the tiniest ways.

I remember when Samantha was a baby, just a few weeks old. She was asleep in her carriage in the garden. Her father and I were sitting out enjoying the sun, but a small nagging concern showed in the crease of my brow as I pondered what we could have to eat. All our money had gone for food for the baby. My husband, never one to worry about such matters, knew without saying that I would come up with something, and I knew there was no point in asking him for help.

"At least we have bread," I thought, "and margarine. Nothing to make a sandwich. I'll just have to toast the bread—then it won't be too bad." I had long since become used to being hungry, and found it easy to ignore my aching stomach now.

The clock ticked by, Samantha slept, and at five o'clock my husband lifted his head to inquire what was for dinner.

"Well," I said, laughing, desperate to stay cheerful, "you have a choice. Bread and margarine, or toast and margarine. I prefer toast myself. How about you?" I looked at him and he nodded and shrugged, and wearily I got up and walked up to the house, looking longingly over the garden fence as I did so. My neighbor Kathy's husband grew vegetables. What I wouldn't have given right then for an onion or two.

I was so engrossed in my thoughts that I wasn't aware of Kathy until she called my name, and then, looking up, I saw my neighbor standing in her garden.

I smiled a greeting, but my smile froze on my face when I heard her next words. Waving her hand over the garden, she said, "Would you like a lettuce, Rosemary? We have so many, and if we don't pick them they'll go to waste."

A lettuce, a lettuce, of course I'd like a lettuce. But I was so proud, and I heard myself saying in such a casual manner, "Oh no, thank you, Kathy, I couldn't, but thank you all the same."

But she insisted. Thank God she insisted. As she pushed the roundest, plumpest lettuce I had ever seen into my hands, I mumbled with quiet dignity, "Well, if you're sure."

With careful nonchalance I walked the rest of the way up the garden and into the house. Gently I closed the door, and only then, in sheer relief, I let out the loudest yell, threw the lettuce in the air, and as I caught it I held it to me saying, "Thank God . . . lettuce sandwiches for tea." Thank God. . . . for miracles!

We all have these small daily occurrences, every one of us, I believe, and it's just a matter of being able to recognize them for what they are. Small miracles, to be valued no less than the greater ones. As I write I remember a story told to me long ago by Betty and Joan Burkett, two spinster sisters who helped run the church I attended. I was perhaps fourteen or fifteen years old at the time.

Betty, the quieter and more timid of the sisters, was home, doing nothing in particular, just puttering. It was, as I remember, a weekday morning at about eleven o'clock when she heard the voice: "Get ice, get ice, and take it to the church."

Betty, startled, looked around, but there was no one there. And the voice came again, this time more urgently: "Get ice, get ice, and take it to the church."

"But, but..." she stuttered, "the church is over three miles away, and I only have my bike. The ice will melt."

For the third time, and most firmly now, the voice came again, saying the same thing. So strong was Betty's faith, she knew this was the voice of God, and hesitating no longer, she went to the kitchen and filled a bag with ice from the freezer. She mounted her bike and raced to the church. She had gone less than two miles when a woman, racing out of her house, screaming and waving her arms, practically threw herself in Betty's path.

"My husband," she gasped, "my husband, he's had an accident. Help me, help us, we need ice, we need ice." And so Betty handed her the ice.

Miracles ... miracles ... miracles ... miracles ...

Does my life run smoothly? No, it does not. My learning, my growing, is still taking place, just like everyone else's. But over the years I have learned to trust a little more. I have learned that no matter what, those in the spirit world, those who love me, my angels, and my guide, will always be there to help and guide me, to keep me safe, and to help me, if I need them, to learn my lessons.

I said at the beginning of this chapter that there is not one question we can ask that somewhere, deep within the recesses of our soul, we do not have the answer to.

And I, just like you, am on a journey of discovery. I must access my soul, and I am aware that my lessons in life, no matter how hard, will lead me to find the key.

One thing I have learned, through all of my past experiences, and my continuing experiences, is that God does truly have a voice.

They Are
Only Children

When God intervenes in our lives, we say, "It's a miracle," and I would be the first to say such a thing, as you know from reading the last chapter. But what is it when a human voice intervenes? Do we call it interference? Would we see that person as a busybody? We certainly don't see God in this light. I have never heard anyone refer to him as a busybody. Why? Because he is all-knowing? Because he gives with love? Because he cares? But there are times when we who are of the earth plane must intervene and say, "I am a member of the human race, and in part, responsible for the human race."

Last night at dinner, I sat with friends discussing our human race. "Nowhere on this earth is there another creature," declared Cook, "who commits atrocities and cruelty to its own kind as we humans do, and have done, over the centuries, since time began." He continued. "We have raped, pillaged, tortured in terrible ways, our fellow man, and even today"—this, referring to the Bosnian conflict—"man is just as cruel, just as mean and mean-spirited, as he was all those centuries ago, in the beginning."

I knew he was right. How could I argue with the facts, terrible and frightening, of what is happening in our world today?

I wanted to argue, to say yes, but we are learning, but we are more enlightened now, but we are growing spiritually ... but ... but ... but ... In my heart, however, I knew it to be the truth that for all the learning and the growing, for all the talk of gentleness, we who are of the human race have so very far to go.

It seemed hopeless to say more, and, saddened, I went to bed.

But morning came. With it came the sun, and as I looked out the window, down into the valley, across to the mountains, the green mountains of Vermont, where I was staying, I felt light enter my heart. I listened, as the heartbeat of my soul pulsed strong within me, and I was filled with hope.

"We have to start somewhere," I whispered to my soul, and remembering that I am a teacher, remembering that I am a member of the human race, that I am not cruel, that there are more of us who are not cruel, that if we can somehow join together, unite in our goal, understand that sometimes it is right to "interfere" or "intervene," and to do this by God's example, with love, then perhaps we can each give, or produce, our own small miracles.

If we could only understand that to sit quietly by and watch injustice meted out ... but, well, each must judge by himself. . . .

It was a holiday weekend, and my friend Kay and I had decided to go out for the day. Kay's three girls, Anna, Chloe, and Jessica, aged sixteen, thirteen, and eight years, came with us. We went to look around the house and gardens of one of England's old historic abbeys, Rufford Park.

It was a lovely day, the sun was shining, the flowers in the gardens were beautiful. Even though there was quite a crowd of people, mostly families, nothing could detract from the splendor of the day. Until, that is, we went for lunch.

There was a large restaurant on the grounds of the house. It was busy and noisy, but clean, and the food was good: homemade cakes and pastries, fresh salads, something to suit everyone. The girls found a table while Kay and I saw to the food and drink.

We were all famished, so we ate heartily, chatting and laughing as we did, as were most of the families around us.

It was as we were coming to the end of our meal that my attention was drawn to another table nearby. At the table sat a young man in his teens, a woman, heavily built, in her early forties, and a small child, a girl, about four years old. I presumed—rightly it turned out—that the woman was the mother of the little girl, and as I listened to her, she reminded me, in the way she spoke to her daughter, of my own mother. Harsh, aggressive, almost brutal. "Watch that drink...Sit on yer chair properly, and stop ya fidgeting," she barked at the child.

I watched and listened, feeling sad for the child and for the mother who was missing so much, wishing for some gentleness. Then I saw the child try to lift herself up onto the table for her drink. Unable to reach, she sat back in her chair, but the bucket-shaped chair was plastic and somewhat slippery, and as the girl sat back she slid down in the chair and cracked her chin hard on the table before tumbling onto the floor. She screamed out in pain and shock, over and over.

This should have been the moment for her mother to gather her up in her arms and comfort her. Instead, the mother, furious at what she saw to be the child's stupidity, yanked her up by her arm. Yelling loud enough for the entire restaurant to hear, she shook the child over and over, calling her stupid, saying, "Shut up, or I'll give yer something to cry for."

I sat and watched, as did everyone else, and saw the child, now totally distraught, push away from her mother and run the length of the room to the door, screaming, "I want my grandma!" The mother, screamed after her, "Go on then, ya little bugger! Go find your grandma! Go on, clear off!" Then she muttered to the young man who was with her, "Stupid little sod. She can go to her grandma."

While this had been going on the restaurant had become silent, all eyes on the scene. Now people were suddenly busy, uncomfortable perhaps, embarrassed, unsure what to do, many disgusted, muttering to one another. I watched as the mother of the child gathered up her belongings and headed to the door.

My friend Kay and her girls were shocked. Kay was angry, the girls distressed. They were not used to seeing such foul abuse. That it was directed toward a child only made it worse.

But I was used to it. I had seen it all before, not just once, but over and over again. This was my childhood, being replayed before my eyes, with one difference: I had had no one to run to.

How many seconds, or even split seconds does it take for memories to flood into our minds. And not just memories, but thoughts of how and why . . . and then, as I sat there, the thought: What could I do about it, what could I do?

Split seconds, and my anger subsided, the anger that I had felt toward this woman, and in its place, determination. Split seconds, and hardly a conscious thought, as I stood, and quietly saying to Kay, "Stay here with the girls for a few minutes, will you?" I headed after the woman, to the door.

I caught up with her just outside the restaurant. The child was nowhere to be seen. Placing my hand on her arm, I firmly turned her to face me and said, "Excuse me, I would like to talk to you for just a moment. It's about the scene in the restaurant back there. You know," I continued, as I looked directly into her eyes, my voice calm, quiet, gentle but firm, "she is just a small child, only a little girl, and she needs gentleness. Please don't scream and yell at her like that. Please be more gentle with her. She is only a small child, just a little girl, and she needs your love."

The woman stood silent, her mouth open in surprise as I spoke to her. Disarmed for a moment by the quiet, gentle way that I had spoken to her, she could not respond. But as I walked away, Grandma, a very large lady with a brood of kids in tow, headed toward us, and seeing her daughter standing gaping after me called out, "What's up with you standing there with yer mouth open?" At that, the woman came alive, and waving her arms about in my direction, screamed loud enough once again for all to hear, "It's her, it's her! Who does she bloody well think she is, telling me how to treat me kids?"

I sighed, turned back, and headed to where the two women stood, my manner now less gentle, as I intended to tell them both exactly who I was.

Perhaps it was something about the set of my jaw that warned her, or perhaps she noted the way I walked toward her, my step unfaltering, my determination showing. I'll never know. But as I came close and stared into her face, she became silent, grabbed hold of her mother's arm, and turned and fled.

I cannot deny that I was grateful, for I really had not relished a fight, but I knew I would have stood my ground, for I had no choice.

"Who does she think she is?" she had yelled. And what would I have said?

"I am a member of the human race, and in my life I have seen many injustices, and I have often stood by silently. In my life I have, from time to time, been unjust, yelled at my child for no good reason, screamed when I should have been silent, judged when I had no right, been mean when I should have been gentle."

And what more would I have said?

"I have been you, and I have been your child, and I will try not to judge. But I am a member of the human race. I am responsible for this earth and for the world we live in, and I will try for the rest of my life never to sit quietly by again when I see injustice meted out."

And I remember the question I asked my guide when we talked about our world, this earth of ours, where anger and frustration seem to know no limits. Where violence and aggression rule. A world where dog eats dog.

I asked the question: "Does it have to be like this?"

Grey Eagle answered... "No... but each man, each woman, each child, must do his or her part."

Again, I hear his voice... "Each individual, each man, woman and child, is the mother of the world, will cradle the world, and will dictate its destiny."... And will dictate its destiny.

It is so hard to live in a spiritual way. We know what is right, what we should do, how we should behave. Our heart tells us, our conscience tells us, our soul tells us. But society often tells us differently. If we speak out we can be seen as troublemakers, agitators even.

History shows that those individuals who did not conform or who dared to speak out against injustice were often at best ostracized, at worst put to death. The Christians who were thrown into the lions' den. Healers and psychics labeled heretics, burned at the stake. The Jews in Nazi Germany and their supporters, stripped of their livelihood, sent into camps, slaughtered in the gas chambers. Martin Luther King, assassinated. Let's face it, which one of us wants to be a hero?

I heard a terrible story several years ago about a man who went to the aid of another man, a stranger, who was being attacked by a gang of thugs with razor blades. For his trouble, the first man was badly beaten, then, as some of the gang sat on him, others proceeded to slice the tendons of his hands, cutting between each finger through to the knuckles. Both men lay in the hospital together later. One had been blinded, the other, the "Good Samaritan," would never be able to use his hands again.

Another story. My daughter's friend Peter was set upon, again by a gang of thugs. They didn't like his haircut, and so they used his head as a football. He almost died, and came out of the hospital with a metal plate in his head.

And more recently, a young man was killed, beaten to death, after going to help a neighbor.

There are many stories like these, many...many...many... too many.

So who wants to be a hero? Who wants to be different? Which of us dares?

But if there was a collective voice...am I being a realist? Is it too simple to say that if all those people in Germany who heard and saw things they knew were bad, knew were evil, if they had from the very beginning dared to say no, if they had stood together, that evil could have been stopped? Could Hitler have been stopped?

I want to say yes. I want to believe yes.

How often is a crime committed, a murder done, a rape, How often is a wife beaten, a child abused, a dog kicked, while neighbors listen? When did you last see a motorist scream at another motorist and think nothing of it except "That's life, life in the city"? And when did you last feel such despair of this society we live in that you felt you must do something about it? Even if that something was just a small prayer asking God's help that you might be a voice that said *no*.

And I struggle as I write this, because I am aware that I begin to sound as if I am preaching and self-righteous. But God knows that I am not, that I have no right to be. For I have stood silent when I knew my voice was needed. I have been one who has turned a blind eye, refused to see, or believed I could do nothing, say nothing, that would make a difference. But I have been wrong.

Again I hear Grey Eagle's voice..."Each man, each woman, each child must do his or her part. It is for you to choose, and you...and you...and you."

I think that we all appreciate what it is that I have been trying to say, but most of us believe that it is not our right to "interfere." So when we sit in an office, as a friend of mine did, and listen to a colleague constantly berate, intimidate, and abuse his timid secretary, we don't like it, we might sympathize with the secretary, but we don't say no. Because we feel it's not our business. Or when an aggressive shopper verbally attacks a shop assistant, or the bus driver yells at a passenger, or the teacher bullies a child . . . we don't like it, we may sympathize . . . but we don't say No. Because "It's not our business." Is it really not our business? The truth, of course, is that it really is.

This is a call to arms. A call from one who has known better, who has often not done the right thing, but who will try for the rest of her life to do what is right. And as Grey Eagle has taught me . . . all that God and the universe require from us is that we try.

There is one more story I would like to tell you. This story is personal and special to me, and I feel it must be told.

Jim had been skiing at Stratton, Vermont, with friends of mine, Joann and Kenny. They had had a great morning and had decided to stop for lunch at the mountain restaurant, the Mid Station.

You can imagine the scene. Skis, boots, noise, chatter, everyone there a skier, lots of people, lots of kids with bright eyes and red noses. A place of fun. Joann, Kenny, and their two children, Jenny and Colin, and Jim found a table and ate a good lunch, enjoying the atmosphere and each other's company.

As lunch was almost over, Joann became aware of a commotion at the table next to theirs, where three children sat with their father. One of the kids, a boy of about ten years old, was being heavily chastised by his father, and he sat, head down, red-faced with embarrassment, and sobbing, as his father, in a loud and bullying tone, berated his son for not being at their designated meeting place on time.

"What time did I tell you to be here? And what time is it? Who do you think you are?" he yelled. The boy tried to explain, but the father wouldn't listen, talking right over the boy, pointing a finger in his face, shouting louder and louder.

Now, obviously the father had a point. As a parent I know that in a place like Stratton, busy, full of strangers, if you lose your child, twenty minutes can seem like a lifetime. And when we are worried, as this father undoubtedly was, yelling at the child can be a natural reaction. It is like releasing a valve—steam comes out.

However, the father continued to scold his son, and his criticism became hypercriticism. As his diatribe continued, his tone became jeering. Reaching over to the boy, he forced a paper napkin, which the child had been holding to his face, away from him. "Don't think you can hide behind that," he snapped. "I want everyone here to see your face, I want them to know what you did. I don't care if you're embarrassed."

On and on it went, to such a point that Joann became very agitated, getting more and more upset for the boy, and for the other kids at the table.

So far, Jim was unaware of all this, but turning from other friends who had come by the table to say something to Joann, he noticed how upset she seemed.

"What's wrong?" he asked.

"Just listen to that man," replied Joann. "He has no right to speak to his son like that. I feel I should do something."

Jim looked over at the table, and at the same moment the boy looked up and into Jim's face. His face was flaming red, and great teardrops ran down his cheeks. As Jim listened, the father's voice continued, unrelenting, jeering, taunting, loud enough so all could hear, deliberately so.

Jim rose, approached the table, and, keeping a fair distance from the man, spoke in a strong but measured voice.

"I think that's enough now," he said. "I'd appreciate it if you would leave the boy alone."

"Listen," said the father arrogantly, caught off guard, "this is none of your business, so stay out of it. He was late and I'm dealing with him."

"I don't care what he did," said Jim, maintaining control. "He's just a child, and you're upsetting him, and a lot of other people too. So just cut it out."

The boy was streaming huge tears, and everyone around was

staring at him. His brother and sister had been sitting with their heads down, also embarrassed, but possibly used to their father making a scene.

Joann had gone to stand at Jim's side, and now the two of them, having finished lunch, headed out into the snow. The father of the boy leaped up and ran outside after Jim and began ranting and yelling, looking for a fight.

"Who the hell do you think you are?" he screamed at Jim. "What the hell has it got to do with you how I treat my kids?" He raised his fists and made as if to hit Jim.

"I'll tell you what it has to do with me," said Jim, "Kids are my business, everybody's business, and I won't stand by and see them abused."

With that, he leaned closer to the father of the boy. "Go ahead, hit me," he said. "You like to pick on little people. Why don't you pick on someone your own size? Go ahead, hit me. I'll be the last person you hit."

The bully backed off. Someone had finally faced him down, and he turned, stumbling, and with his tail between his legs, went back into the restaurant.

I was in England when this happened, having just returned from Vermont myself. It was Joann who called and told me the story— a story much like my own about the woman and her daughter that I recounted at the beginning of this chapter.

As she told me of her experience, Joann was obviously tremendously impressed, and not just by seeing Jim as a champion, a defender of right action. She was also impressed by the control Jim had displayed when dealing with the father outside in the snow.

Several hours later I spoke to Jim, and I asked him about the incident.

His voice somber, he replied, "I am not sorry I did what I did. The father was a bully and I had to say something. But I am sorry for the way I reacted outside. I was angry, and I wanted him to hit me, because I just really would have liked to punch him on the nose, and that was wrong, and I feel embarrassed and ashamed. I could have handled it better, and I didn't."

When Joann first told me this story I felt proud that I should know this defender of children, a man who felt strongly enough to stand and be counted. But it was as I heard him say that he was ashamed of his own aggression, it was as I heard his own humility shine through and saw that he truly understood the need for gentleness even in difficult circumstances, that I knew how right I was to love this man. And I felt tremendous pride that he should love me too.

Crowning
Glory

In recounting the last story, I began to reflect upon my own feelings, and it was as I did this that I realized my overriding emotion was compassion. I felt compassion for the child whose father had screamed at him. But more, I felt compassion for the father, for his need to scream and yell, for his need to bully. I felt compassion for his confusion and for the joys in life he was, at that moment, so obviously unaware of.

Will he grow old regretting his actions, his behavior? And what of the child? Will he grow older learning to bully, as his father taught him, or by some small miracle, will he remember his pain, and learn compassion?

Our childhood experiences can be powerful teachers, as this next story shows.

The only sound in the room was the snip, snip, snip of the scissors. Woe betide me if I cried. Tears rained silent and salty down my cheeks. The sound grew louder: snip, snip, snip.

I was eleven years old. My hair, like all my sisters', was long, way down my back, my crowning glory. We always had to wear it in braids, and earlier that day my father had been brushing it in his usual rough way and I had cried out one time too many as he tried to get the tangles out.

It didn't take long, hardly any time at all.

The sound changed.

Now the clippers, as he shaved the back of my head.

"Now you'll have something to cry about," he said as he brutally pushed me out of the chair.

I can still see their faces as they grinned. My family.

At school it was easy. I lied. We had been reading an Enid Blyton novel, *The Famous Five.* One of the characters, Georgina, hated being a girl. She wore boy's clothes and kept her hair short. I told my friends I wanted to be like her, and it wasn't long before they started calling me George.

Everywhere else I went—to the Girl Guides, to church—I wore one of my mother's silk squares wrapped tightly around my head so it wouldn't slip off, refusing to take it off except at home. It seemed like an eternity till my hair grew again.

> *Oh the pain and oh the suffering*
> *Humiliation, raw and bleeding*
> *All these lessons, meant to teach us*
> *All these trials, meant to mold us*

These words, going round in my head, as memory stirs, and old feelings return. So what did I learn, I ask myself, all anger gone and only a shadow of the pain left to remind me of this childhood hurt.

It was well past midnight when the phone rang. I was not asleep, just nicely relaxed, as I picked it up, but I was instantly alert as her hysterical cries and screams met my ears. "Help me, help me, don't let him die," she screamed at me, over and over.

At first gently, then my voice sharp, I tried to break through the hysteria and understand her.

97

Her son was eight years old. He had been diagnosed with cancer when he was five, three years previously. After surgery and many different kinds of treatment the doctors had finally given up. Only a miracle can save him now, she was told. And so she called me.

I knew as I listened to her that the miracle she wanted was not one I could give. It was his time. That instinct born to me told me it was his time.

"You must see him," she begged. "You must help us. Please, please, just see him."

Such a long time ago now, more than fifteen years. Mark was my first child patient, and I prayed to God that I could give him something, just some small part of me that might somehow help him and his mother in their pain.

He was so small and thin, far too small for his age. And so pale, sickly white. His dark eyes gazed out at me with only the slightest interest.

But the most shocking sight for me was that this child had no hair. He had lost it through his treatment.

Faint memory stirred. Instinctively my hand went to my head. I stood then for a moment, remembering.

Oh the pain and oh the suffering
Humiliation, raw and bleeding
All these lessons, meant to teach us
All these trials, meant to mold us

Mark died a few days later. He joined the many children who die. And we who are left behind ask why.

I would like to be able to tell you that I have seen Mark since he passed, but that wouldn't be true, unless, of course, he is among the many children who have visited me over the years, all safe, all well and happy, with bright eyes and shining hair. I see them clearly. Angels all. They are tomorrow's children, and tomorrow's, and tomorrow's, and tomorrow's.

Instinctively I lift my hand to touch my hair, remembering back.

And so what did I learn? I ask myself, all anger gone, and only a shadow of the pain left to remind me of this childhood hurt.

I learned compassion.

It is odd, don't you think, how childhood memories can be stored, laid dormant somewhere in the recesses of our brain, waiting for some experience, a smell, a touch, the sound of a voice...some trigger which explodes the memory, bringing it, often with startling clarity, to the forefront of our minds.

It was through Mark that I remembered my childhood hurt, but it was through another source that I more recently remembered Mark, and I wrote Mark's story somehow as a tribute to this organization, Tomorrow's Children.

I first became aware of them when I was at a bookstore in New Jersey in October 1995. Having given a talk to my audience of several hundred, I began to sign books. The line was a long one, and although I was thrilled to see how many people had been inspired to buy my first book, *The Eagle and the Rose*, nevertheless I was very tired. And I knew the signing was going to take a while, as each person in line had something to say to me. Try as I might, time was short, and I am only one person. I could not give to each one as much as I would have liked. I knew that there were many who, desperate for a word with a departed loved one, saw an opportunity, only to be disappointed. Many were openly crying, and although my heart went out to them in their pain, there was little I could give but a look of compassion.

One couple particularly caught at my heartstrings. While I was signing their book they told me they had lost their child. They held on to each other so tightly and her look was so desperate I suggested that if they were prepared to wait until I had finished signing I would speak with them for just a few moments.

For a while I forgot about them, and it must have been an

hour later, my hand cramped with writing, that I finished the signing and gave my attention over to them. I had asked another woman to join them. She was in a wheelchair and her eight-year-old son was close by her in attendance. I knew that this woman had also lost a child.

Fortunately, there were large comfortable chairs in this bookstore, and as I headed for one, an assistant from the store brought me a much-needed drink. The first couple asked if two friends could join us, and I had no objection. They and the woman in the wheelchair and her son drew close. We made a tight little group, joined together by grief, and by hope.

I reached my arms out to the boy and asked him to come sit with me in the chair. As I held him on my knee, I could feel his pain and could sense the struggle he had as he bravely held his emotions in check, trying to be strong for his mother's sake, but desperate in his grief for the loss of his brother.

It was the greatest gift to me that night as this boy's brother, only three or four years old, came through from the spirit world to give message after message of hope and reassurance to his brother and his mother. My arms closed gently about this eight-year-old as I gave one final message. I heard his brother say quite clearly, "Tell him I'm his angel now, and that I will be with him always."

My attention was then held, not by the couple who were waiting so patiently, but by a little girl from the spirit world, so dainty, so sweet, but not quite as patient as her parents had been. "My turn now, my turn now," I heard her say, and smiling, I agreed, she had waited long enough. It was her turn. She told me how she had died of cancer, how horrible it had been, and how much she had cried when the pain came. That was hard for her parents to hear. But having explained that, this fairy child went on to describe many things, giving evidence to her parents of her survival after death. Soon we were all laughing at her antics as she made it clear to her parents that she was watching them, and that she was alive.

At some point during my conversation with this child I noticed that there were many people sitting quietly nearby, watching me work, seeing the effects of my work. They had come to the bookstore to hear me speak and get their books signed, and then had become aware of this "other happening." Without being intrusive, they had wanted in some way to be part of it. They could not hear all that was said, but they obviously sensed that something wonderful and special was happening and wanted in some small way to share in it.

Thinking of this afterward, I felt there had been a kind of reverence, a feeling of holiness and sanctity, pervading us all, and I was sure that we had all been aware of God's infinite presence.

The fairy child continued to talk to her parents, and mentioning Christmas, assured them that she would be with them on that holiday occasion.

It was well over an hour later that I suddenly became aware of my strength ebbing. A small throbbing in my head, a dull ache, reminded me how tired I was, and I knew the session must come to an end.

The child's parents, moved to tears, thanked me, and then told me of the organization to which they belonged, an organization that had raised funds and built a hospital for children with rare cancers. This organization also ran a support group for the families of these children. I was instantly interested, and so when they asked if I would go and speak to this group, without hesitation I agreed.

Two weeks before Christmas, on December 11, my friend Joann and I made our way over to Hackensack, New Jersey. We arrived at the hospital in freezing snow and were ushered into the warmth of one of the hospital lounges. Sitting around the room on hard-backed chairs were approximately thirty-five people, men and women, parents who had lost their children. In the middle of the room were two large coffee tables supporting plates of sandwiches and cakes.

My first thought on entering was "Oh no, I am never going to be able to satisfy all these people." I thought, hoped, that we might make contact with perhaps three or four children. Given the time we had (I had agreed to give a two-hour talk), I couldn't expect more than that. Unfortunately, these people would not be satisfied hearing from someone else's child, even if it was a child they had known. They wanted to hear from their own, which was perfectly understandable.

Prior to my coming to this group I had made it plain to them, as I always do before any lecture, that I cannot ever say what will happen. I can never guarantee that spirit contact will be made, and it was with a reminder of this to them that I began to work.

To my delight it was not long before I heard a voice, my first contact, and I became aware of a boy from the spirit world standing behind me wanting to speak to Tom.

"I'm Tom," said the man sitting next to me.

"I'm hearing the name David," I went on to say. A couple sitting to my right, farther round the room said, "Oh, that's us."

Well, I was quite confused. It seemed that I had two boys from the spirit world talking to me at the same time. It took a while to sort things out, and the minutes were ticking by.

But I need not have worried, for one by one, and slowly going to each person in the room, children from the spirit world came through to talk to their parents.

One child, a little girl, describing the dental treatment her mother had just had. Another child talking of how he had watched his parents move house. A daughter who, having described how she died, and putting her arms around her parents, told us how proud she was that her dad had won a silver cup in a golf tournament. He told us later that he had received his silver cup the previous Saturday, and yes, for playing golf.

On and on we went, around the room, until everyone there had received a message from his or her beloved child.

I was thrilled. No one had been missed. Of course, it is too much to hope that everyone in that room became a total believer, even though the hard evidence each one had received could not easily be dismissed. But I think it fair to say that most were convinced that their children had been present, that there was indeed communication. One or two, I am sure, remained skeptical, but must at least have concluded that contact with those in the spirit world might be just more than possible.

As for me, well, my responsibilities to those children who had "died" had been fulfilled. My concerns, always for those in the spirit world first, had been addressed. I had been their voice, I had been their messenger—not perfect, but the best that I could be.

That I had given something to their parents was a pleasure to me, but a secondary concern. That I had given to the children was an honor and a joy.

It was time to end this session. I looked to the child who had brought me here, the little girl I had first talked with in the bookstore. She was ready now to give one more message, a message not just from her to her parents, she told me, but a message from all of the children there to their mothers and their fathers.

I smiled at this fairy child and repeated her words as she spoke to me. "And it's Christmas," she said, "and on Christmas morning, when you wake, open your eyes and look to the brightest place in the room, for that is where we will be. You might hear us calling, 'Merry Christmas, Mommy, Merry Christmas, Daddy.' And we will smile and be happy knowing that you can see our light."

I looked again into the eyes of this fairy child, and then, slowly I turned to each of the children there in the room, my eyes reaching the eyes of each child, my smile acknowledging their smile, as each in turn gave me their thanks. And I knew peace as I gathered them to me and gave them my love, as they gave me theirs, for here truly were Tomorrow's Children, safe with God.

And there was one last message the fairy child gave, and I smiled as I heard her words:

"Oh yes," she said, and I watched as the light danced around her. "God says hello."

Part III

A JOURNEY
TOWARD HEALING

THERE ARE MANY DIFFERENT KINDS OF HEALING, BUT IN THIS SEC-tion, we are concerned only with spiritual healing, given most often in the form of a laying on of hands, such as Christ did, but as you will see, sometimes given in other ways.

Before we begin, let me first explain how we in my organization, the Rosemary Altea Association of Healers, perceive the healing art. I, as the founder and teacher of this group, would like to share with you my thoughts and feelings about spiritual healing.

To do this, first I must explain that every living thing has an aura. Our aura, or energy field, surrounds us, extending above and beyond the skin by several feet. This energy field can be photographed, using a special camera developed by a Russian couple, Semyon and Valentina Kirlean, many years ago.

The soul too has its aura, its energy field, and we refer to this energy as the spirit, the light that surrounds and gives light to the soul.

When we become physically sick, our ill health is mirrored in our aura, affects our aura, often affects our spirit. When the soul becomes needy, this too reflects in the soul's aura, our spirit, which will often dim. The light will become less, and the soul will struggle in the dark.

So when we give healing, first we ask for God's help, for his energy, for his light, and we ask that this energy be given first to the spirit, so that the soul's aura can become brighter and give more light to the soul. When this happens, a great healing will take place. When the soul absorbs that healing energy, and when the soul finds that peace and enlightenment it so needs, then, often, a physical healing will take place.

So a spiritual healer will look first to give healing to the spirit, the light of the soul. Not, as many suppose, to the cancer, to the arthritis, to the migraine, but first to the spirit, which in turn, if God chooses, will heal us physically.

I begin this section, "A Journey Toward Healing," with a question from my guide, Grey Eagle, who is himself a healer, a shaman. This question, asked by so many, so often, and by me also, is answered in a way which will, I hope, allow you insight into the most important message, especially for those who are sick and dying and for those who are about to lose someone to sickness. ... this message is that we don't die, that we are soul ... and that we truly live on.

Question

Question: Grey Eagle, why does spiritual healing cure some and not others?

Answer: A human soul reaches out toward another human soul, with love and compassion its only tools. It touches the heart of that other human soul, and the soul of that one which is distressed will acknowledge and respond to that touch of love ... will embrace it and will grow from it.

There is not one who touches another with love who does not succeed in giving healing to the soul.

To answer your question, we must, again, address your concept of death ... your concept of well-being. A child of God crippled in his physical body may have a spirit which is light, which soars through the heavens, which is free. This soul accepts and knows that the vehicle in which it chooses to be encased is a vehicle for a short time only.

All who look toward the light . . . the crippled . . . the lame . . . the distressed . . . the anxious . . . all can experience this gift of healing.

When the physical form dies, we hear you say, "He died, there was no cure." But is death not a cure? For is not the soul then released, to continue to grow . . . to live . . . to feel . . . to be?

And, so, I will tell you, and truly from my heart, the cure that *you* seek may not be the cure that God knows is best for the soul . . . may not be the cure that the soul knows is best for the soul.

And we recognize, with your limited vision, you may only begin to glimpse the truth of what I say to you.

Chris

I was a medium, a spiritual medium, and my friend Mick McGuire, well, he was the healer. We both had our separate roles, and I was happy. "I could never be a healer," I had thought often. "And furthermore, sickness terrifies me. I would never be strong enough. Thank God I wasn't chosen to do this work."

How they must have laughed, though gentle laughter I am sure, those in the spirit world who knew my thoughts. And as they guided me and gently steered me to the role they knew was already mine, how they cared for me. They gave me firm but gentle teaching.

It has been many years now since I began the RAAH, the Rosemary Altea Association of Healers. We opened our first center in 1986, and since that time my team and I have developed a small but dedicated organization with patients around the world.

The first time I visited Hong Kong I stayed for six weeks, and each time after that my stays grew longer and my clientele grew. It had been at the invitation of one of my clients, Kay Frost, that I first came to visit the Far East. Kay and her husband, Peter, had moved to Hong Kong from England when Peter had been promoted by his company. It had been a major decision for them both as they had two children, Charlotte and young Peter, to consider, and Kay had first come to consult me about this change. She had wanted to know if moving was the right thing to do, would the children be okay, and so on. To me, Kay was just another client, and so when she came to see me for a second time (she was in England for two weeks visiting family) and invited me to visit Hong Kong, to stay and to work from her home there, I really did not take the invitation too seriously.

Several letters and a couple of phone calls later I realized that not only was she persistent, but she was generously offering me the chance of a lifetime. With no desire or thought of gain for herself, she genuinely wanted to give me the opportunity to widen my horizons in respect to my work. During her second phone call to me, on the spur of the moment, and with no thought whatsoever, I said yes. This was the beginning of my travels, and as word spread of my work, my clientele grew, as did my list of patients.

Pretty soon I was almost as involved with healing in Hong Kong as I was in England, and I found myself with a very heavy workload, for unlike my situation in England, where I had a team of healers working with me, able to support me, here in Hong Kong I was alone.

One of my first patients was Lynne, an American woman who, when I first met her, had been undergoing treatment for cancer for about two years. It was with Lynne that I made my first visit to the United States. I had stayed at her house in Hong Kong for several weeks, and she and her husband, Geoff, had become my firm friends.

Lynne first heard me on a radio show, being interviewed by Valerie Whitehead, the presenter of one of the most popular morning radio shows in Hong Kong. I was talking about healing, and at one point in the show, I mentioned that I really needed to find a venue in Hong Kong where people could come and have a healing experience. The response was amazing, and many people offered their homes and offices. Lynne was one of these, and so we set up an evening once a week in Lynne's home where patients could come, free of charge.

The radio show was also my means of meeting Chris. A young man in his early forties, with a wife and two young children, he had been diagnosed as having growths on his lungs, not malignant, but deadly, as they were inoperable and growing larger. We first met in the foyer of one of the fancier hotels in Hong Kong, and as total strangers, we rode up in the elevator to an apartment which belonged to one of Chris's friends. After an hour-long healing session, we became good friends. Chris had many healing sessions with me, but the one that stands out most vividly in my mind occurred after he had taken me to visit Dr. Woo. Dr. Woo, a Buddhist priest who practiced as a doctor of herbal remedies, was also treating Chris. He was an incredible man, somewhere in his late seventies or early eighties, but sprightly and intelligent. He would sit cross-legged on a small rickety stool, certainly something I was not agile enough to do, and study his patient, asking a few questions, before making his diagnosis and deciding upon the appropriate treatment.

I was his patient this day, and although his questions were few, brief and seemingly vague, he did tell me about the problem I was having with my stomach. He was also quite accurate when he described the situation with my kidneys. However, impressed as I was, and curious as I was to see what treatment he would prescribe, I found it hard to follow through with his remedy. After I had cooked his herbs, which looked like bits of gnarled tree bark and unspeakable dried insects and grubs dug out of the ground, the stench that came from the muddy liquid made it impossible for me to drink it as I was supposed to. For at the best of times I have a sensitive stomach, and my retching, every time I came close enough to take even the smallest sip, put an end to any hope I had of an herbal cure. I hasten to add that not all herbal remedies are like this. On the contrary, many herbal medicines are very easy to take, and they can be very beneficial.

However, I digress. On the day that I first met Dr. Woo, Chris and I went to the herbal pharmacy to have our prescriptions filled. While we waited, Chris asked if I had time for coffee, and so, our small packages in our hands, we made our way through the streets of Wan Chai, a suburb of Hong Kong, looking for a café. As we wound our way through the narrow back streets, noisy with traffic, the overpowering smell of exhaust fumes and fried rice in our nostrils, Chris told me he had hoped I would have time that day to give him healing, but my encounter with Dr. Woo had taken longer than we had thought it would. "And anyway," said Chris, looking around him, "I don't know where we would find a quiet place around here."

At that moment I spied a café, a small, typical Chinese equivalent of a coffee bar with tables out on the street. Shutters the full length of the café had been pulled up, and the café was wide open, allowing all the fumes and dirt from the road and the heavy traffic in. But this was Hong Kong, and this was how it was, and so, almost having to shout to Chris in order to make myself heard over the rumble of trucks and heavy wagons, I suggested, that we try the café.

Chris shrugged and nodded his agreement, knowing that we would have to walk quite a bit farther to find anything better. We sat at the table farthest from the road, which didn't help much, as the café was on a busy corner, and ordered coffee.

"So when is the earliest you could fit me in for a healing session, Rosemary?" Chris asked while we sipped our drinks.

"Well, how about now?" I asked. "I'll have my coffee and then, if it's okay with you, we can begin."

"What?" replied Chris, startled. "You mean here, now, with all this going on?" He waved his hands to indicate the commotion in full flow around us.

I laughed and replied that although we were not exactly in the most ideal setting, beggars couldn't be choosers. If he was willing, so was I.

"Okay," said Chris, a little perplexed, but trusting that I knew what I was doing. And so a few minutes later we began.

Chris moved his chair a little closer to mine so I could reach him easily, and as I laid my hands, my left on his chest, the right on his back, I did as I always do when giving healing—I asked for God's divine help, for his healing energy to be directed toward my patient. There is, I believe, great power in prayer, and I prayed now that my patient's spirit be enhanced with light, and with the love of God, so that his soul would better be able to receive the healing rays of God and the universe which I was sure were at work.

The healer acts as a conduit for that energy, healing energy, which passes through the healer and then on to the patient.

As I have already explained, when spiritual healing is given, it is first directed to the spirit of the patient. The spirit is the light of the soul, which, if bright and pure, gives light and enlightenment to the soul. It is widely accepted in medical circles that stress and emotional disharmony are the greatest killers of the human race, causing many, many physical ailments. The way to rid ourselves of disharmony within us is to ensure that the soul has light, to remember that we are, first and forever, spiritual beings.

How can the soul function and grow without light? It cannot. In the same way a flower bulb needs light and sunshine before it can sprout green leaves and beautiful flowers, the soul needs warmth and light. The spirit, call it the aura or energy field, which surrounds the soul needs only our awareness that it exists to become brighter. And once we are aware of its existence, we can train our thoughts and actions in respect to our spirit, and so the spirit will, given its due and proper attention, become even brighter still, allowing the soul more growth. As we give to the spirit our love and as we become more attentive to its needs, so our mind, body, emotions, and spirit harmonize, allowing us peace and tranquillity.

This is how it was with Chris, as we sat on the seemingly busiest street in Hong Kong, with cars and trucks and noise and fumes all around us. As I laid my hands on him he ceased his questioning thoughts, felt the love of God flow through him, basked in light and quiet solitude as his healing continued, and found peace within it.

Over the months that followed we talked often of that experience, and Chris would remark that it was one of the best healing sessions he ever had. It also changed the idea that he and many others have that healing can only be given and received under "proper" conditions. Chris learned that God really is everywhere, and can work his miracle of love anywhere.

Like a bulb, the soul is planted.
In soil, its roots go deep into the earth.
Its only needs, light and love.
And given those, it surely will flower.

Wendy

Perhaps it was with Chris that the first tentative thoughts of a healing tape came into my head, for what could I do for my patient while I was away from him, back home in England?

There were many others too. The old man going blind, and several of my patients with cancer. Bob, whom I first met while he was undergoing treatment in a hospital room in Hong Kong, an American, a man I became very close to. David, a wonderful man, and his wife, Heather. What could I do for them when I returned to England? How could I help them? How could I inspire them to help themselves? Perhaps a tape, a meditation tape, a healing meditation. But such things cost money to produce, and I had no money. So I pushed those thoughts to the back of my mind. "One day," I said to myself, "perhaps one day."

For the next couple of years I traveled back and forth between England and Hong Kong, always busy, often frustrated that I couldn't do more, see more people, as time and the fact that I am only one person seemed to limit my work. And occasionally I would think of my first book, which was mostly written, and of the first healing tape yet to come. "One day," I would muse in an idle moment, usually before sleep. "One day."

My travels to the Far East had broadened my horizons. Having met so many wonderful people, I began to realize how the world was changing, or so it seemed to me, in its view of what used to be termed the "paranormal" and "supernatural." As I traveled I met with more and more open-mindedness, and also, delightedly, not just curiosity, but a genuine and keen interest almost everywhere I went. However, it was on a return visit to England, and through a patient of mine, Wendy, that my first healing tape came into being.

Wendy was my patient for approximately three years. Like so many cancer patients, she had been told by her doctors that there was no hope for her of recovery. That was when she came to one of our healing centers in the north of England. Each week she would arrive, full of determination and fight, and each week she gave to us, even as we gave to her. For there was on her face a ready smile, a word of gratitude, and a willingness to help other patients, to talk to them, and to listen, even in those times when she herself was feeling sick and afraid. I grew more fond of Wendy as time went by. When the time came that she could no longer attend the center, I visited her at home as often as I could.

As always happens in cases like this, I got to know Wendy's husband, Mick, and her two boys, both teenagers at the time, quite well. My visits became a small highlight in all our lives. Tea, biscuits, and long chats, as well, of course, as Wendy's healing sessions, were things we all looked forward to. But with Wendy's illness a constant reminder of why I was there, a small dark shadow, was ever present, and I was constantly looking for ways to ease my patient's mind.

Wendy grew weaker and weaker, and I watched as this brave young woman struggled to hold on to her life. She began to ask me more questions about my beliefs in the afterlife, and about the purpose of life here on earth. Our discussions became deeper and her questions more probing as the last weeks of her life approached.

On one of my visits to see Wendy, her husband, Mick, told me that they had been listening to me do a radio interview that morning. Mick said that he had seen Wendy, who had been terribly sick earlier in the day and unable to get out of bed, become visibly stronger as she heard the sound of my voice, which had seemed to inspire her to find the strength to leave her bed and dress herself in time for my visit that afternoon. "It was amazing," Mick said. "It was as if just hearing your voice was like a healing in itself."

Wendy, who had been listening to her husband tell this story, nodded her agreement, and then said that hearing my voice on the radio was almost as good as having me present.

Thoughts stole into my head. Thoughts of a healing tape, familiar thoughts, not yet put into action. "One day," I had often mused, "One day." And perhaps, I thought as I drove home later, that day has come. But how? My finances were still so low there was no way I could afford to produce a tape. And anyway, even if I could, that wouldn't help Wendy, for I knew her time was drawing close.

I walked into the house somewhat troubled, knowing that Wendy had perhaps no more than four to six weeks left on this earth.

"How can I do more?" I asked Grey Eagle. "What else can I do?"

Then I saw the tape machine, standing on the kitchen table, and I knew what I must do.

Without time to think, I gathered paper and pens and sat down at the table to write, knowing that inspiration would come to me. Without needing to ask, I understood that Grey Eagle would steer my hand, and that he, and God, and my love of Christ, my friend and teacher from the beginning of my life, that greatest of all healers, would work with me, help me, give me the inspiration I needed for a healing meditation.

It took perhaps two hours to write and a little longer to record.

I found a tape of soothing water music, which I played softly in the background, and I spoke the words which would eventually become the first in a series of healing tapes, to be sold around the world.

The next day I took a copy of the tape I'd made to Wendy. She was overjoyed, and played it not just once, but several times a day, until the day she left us. My voice, she said, was a reassurance and helped her find peace. And listening as I described how by visualizing and using certain colors she could give healing to herself, it was, she felt, very beneficial, almost magical.

"Is the color blue really the universal healing color?" she once asked, as I was explaining how many healers use color to enhance the strength of their healing process.

I nodded my answer, and told her that I always, when giving healing, visualize my patients in a protective cloud or bubble of blue. This information helped her too. Often while listening to the tape I had made her she would visualize placing herself inside a blue bubble. As the days wore on and Wendy became weaker and weaker, she also became more serene, more peaceful, more at ease with her fate. Until, that is, one fateful day, just two days before she died.

Wendy was a churchgoer. Her church and her religious beliefs meant a great deal to her. She had great respect for her minister, and when she had first begun to come to us for healing, Wendy had asked him whether she should have healing from us or not. He had led her to believe that he was perfectly happy for her to do so. During the time that Wendy was my patient, still an ardent churchgoer, she had occasionally talked to her minister about her feelings and experiences of healing. Never once had he given her any indication that she was doing something he did not approve of.

Until two days before she died. It was his final visit to her, and this was the time he chose to talk to Wendy about heaven and hell. And it was on this last visit that he chose to tell her that her association with me and with healing was wrong, that it was not of God, and that unless she denounced it all, she would not enter into the Kingdom of God.

Earlier that day, just prior to this man's visit, I had dropped in on Wendy. As I was in the area, visiting other patients, I had promised to call back later. I knew that this might be the last time I would see Wendy, on the earth plane anyway, and I was preparing to say my goodbyes. As I walked into the kitchen I was met by Mick, and I could see immediately that something was very wrong.

Mick was extremely agitated. Although Wendy had not told him what the minister had said, he could see that she was terribly upset. She had insisted that when I came, even if she was asleep, he must wake her up, because she needed to talk to me, and she needed to talk to me alone.

For Wendy's husband to leave the two of us together must have been very hard. He could see his wife's obvious distress, knew that in some way I might be the cause of it, knew he was being shut out of something that was causing pain to Wendy. Loving her as he did, needing to protect her, he must have found it painful to close the bedroom door on us and walk away.

I sat down on the chair next to the bed and held my patient's hand. She looked so small and shrunken, so weak, so frail. She could hardly lift her head from the pillow, let alone speak. And as I write of our conversation, her words and mine etched on my heart forever, I remember her struggle, her determination as she gasped and fought for over an hour to get out words it will take but a moment to repeat.

She told of the minister's visit, of her confusion, of her inability to understand why he hadn't spoken out against me sooner, and of her fear, her mortal fear, that she had done some terrible thing against God and would be damned to hell.

"He told me you were a cheat, a charlatan, and a liar," she said. "I tried to defend you. I told him you were none of those things, that if he met you, talked to you, then he would see for himself. He said he didn't need to see, that you were obviously a fake and spent your life trying to fool people, that what you did was not godly."

I sat quietly, still holding her hand, terribly aware of the distress she was in. Her eyes, large and fearful, never left my face as she recounted all that this "man of God" had said to her. And in my heart I felt a great sadness, for I could see quite clearly that in just one brief moment all of the peace and harmony of the spirit that had been hers had been snatched away. Then—such a painful moment, for I knew she was thinking of me—she asked me this question, ashamed at asking, but desperately needing the truth:

"Is he right, Rosemary? Are you a fake? Is it all just a pretense?" Then, her eyes less fearful and full of compassion for me, and all the while struggling for breath, she said, "It's okay, really it is, you can tell me if he's right. I won't tell. I won't tell Mick, I won't tell anyone, not a soul, I promise. I just need to know the truth." As she said this last sentence, her body slumped and she closed her eyes, but she quickly opened them again. They stayed pinned on my face until I had finished speaking.

Had I been younger, less wise, I might have been indignant, even angry, that someone had dared to suggest that I was a liar, and particularly that I took advantage of the sick and dying, although what benefit he thought I would gain was beyond me, as no one in my healing organization ever charged for services, and money never changed hands. Had I been younger, more of a hot-head, thinking more of my feelings than my patients, I might have said these things to her, I might have felt the need to defend myself, my motives, and my beliefs.

But I did none of these things. Instead, quietly, I told her of my love of God, my faith in Jesus Christ. I told her of my belief that all of us go to God, that the Kingdom of Heaven is not some exclusive club reserved only for those the church of whatever religious body there might be dictates. I explained that I believe all humans err, but we all of us, without exception, are of God, a part of some great God power, a universal plan which embraces us all, believers and nonbelievers alike. I told her that I believe there are many roads leading to God, and that although mine was a little different from others, nevertheless I felt that it was right for me.

"I cannot defend who and what I am, Wendy," I said. "I know who I am, and that is enough for me. If you need to deny me," I continued, smiling and gently squeezing her hand, "then that's okay with me. I will still love you, will still pray for you if I may. But you need to find your peace, your God, and if the minister can help you do this, then don't hesitate."

I watched as tears rolled down her cheeks, and as I wiped them away I said, "God knows best what you need. Trust him, Wendy. He hasn't deserted you, nor will I. I will always be your friend, even if you turn away from me as you might feel you must."

I stayed with her a short while longer, and watched as her eyes closed and a troubled sleep descended. Then I left.

It took me thirty minutes to get back home, and as I drove I cried and cried. I yelled at God, I yelled at Christ, and I yelled at Grey Eagle. And I sobbed, "It's not fair, it's not fair," over and over again.

"All of my patients die in peace, unafraid. That's the rule, that's the compensation, isn't it? Isn't it?" This I said as I paced the hallway later that night, unable to sleep. "That's the compensation, that's what's fair," I yelled again, anger and frustration ebbing and flowing, ebbing and flowing, as I remembered my patient's distress. I was angry at the minister too. How could he have said those things to her at a time when she needed his comfort, his love?

All through the night I paced, and it wasn't until the early hours, when dawn was almost breaking, that I remembered my words to Wendy. My anger and frustration subsided as again I spoke the words out loud . . . but this time, to myself: "God knows best what you need . . . trust him . . . he hasn't deserted you." And

I whispered a prayer: "Help her, Lord, give her what she needs, even if it means she turns away from me. Give her a sign, some small thing, that will ease her heart and give her peace and make her journey a joyful one. Please God in heaven help her, for I know I can do no more."

It was with tears on my pillow that I finally fell asleep. But they were tears of relief, as I had remembered that I am only human and can only do so much. The rest is in God's hands.

I struggled awake just a few hours later. My day was a busy one—clients to see in the morning, patients in the afternoon. My thoughts of Wendy were put to the side as I prepared to see my first client of the day, but just before I began, the telephone rang. It was Wendy's husband, Mick.

"I'm really sorry to bother you, Rosemary, I know how busy you are, but it's Wendy. She woke me at six-thirty this morning insisting that she must speak to you. She wanted me to call you first thing, but I've held off until now. She has to see you, she won't stop asking for you, and she refuses to rest until I can tell her you're coming."

"Don't worry," I said, checking the time. "I'll be there as soon as I can, in midafternoon probably. Is that okay?"

The relief in Mick's voice was obvious as he said how grateful he was. Now he could tell Wendy I was coming, and he felt sure she would settle down.

The Wendy I saw as I walked into her bedroom was not the Wendy of the previous day. She was still extraordinarily weak, still unable to lift her head more than slightly from the pillow, still frail and shrunken. Yet as I looked into her eyes there was a light that danced within them, and a small smile played around her mouth. Again, it takes much less time to tell this story than it took to live it, for her breathing was no less labored, the effort to get the words out no less intense. As before, I held her hand and looked into her eyes as they bored into mine.

"I...saw...it," she whispered, "this...morning...when...I ...woke."

The waiting was endless. Somewhere a clock was ticking. I was aware of its sound as the minutes of my friend's life ticked away, slowly...slowly, and still I waited as she gathered her strength.

"I...opened...my...eyes...and there it was," she finished, in a rush.

"Blue...blue...the...whole...room, filled...with...a... blue...light...so beautiful...it...filled...me...up. So...so ...peaceful...You...were...right...right...a...universal... healing...blue."

Then, strength came to her—from God, I know—and she lifted her head from the pillow and reached out to me. "You must tell them...all...all...what...I...saw." And tears spilled down her face, but she was laughing. Her tears were tears of joy, as she told me once more that she had seen the light of healing, that it had filled up the room and brought her peace.

I remember how she spoke the names of her husband and sons, and the names of her family and close friends. "Not just them," she had said, "not only them, but everyone, tell everyone, for everyone on earth should know."

I stayed with Wendy and her husband, Mick, for several hours that day. At one point, concerned that Mick and the boys should have these last hours with Wendy, and at a moment when we all thought she was asleep, I suggested to Mick that it was time I left, but Wendy opened her eyes and in a strong voice said, "No, Rosemary, not yet, not yet."

So I stayed awhile longer, and just before I left, Wendy opened her eyes again. At first she stared straight past me, her eyes focused on something, or someone, none of us could see. Then her gaze shifted and she looked for a moment right into my eyes. It was then that she gave me the greatest gift. I smile even as tears spring to my eyes, as I write, and I pause a moment, remembering...the

125

brightest smile, so beautiful, so full of light, and I knew my prayer had been answered. God had brought her peace.

After Wendy's funeral, Mick told me that Wendy had left a small sum of money for me. I knew that her intention was that it be used to make a tape, so that others might benefit as she had. I arranged for the healing tape to be produced, and on the allotted day went to the recording studio. Now this sounds much more grand than it actually was—a small room in the house of Mervyn Futter, the man who first produced and also composed the music for the tape, *A Journey Toward Healing*. Mervyn sat in this room with all of the recording equipment, and I, sitting on a high stool, a microphone on a stand, sat in the hallway, a set of headphones on my head.

"Okay," I heard Mervyn say, "try not to rustle any papers, and we can begin."

On my lap I held the written script, and as I looked down to check it one more time I automatically spoke to my guide, asking for his help. Then I took a deep breath, feeling ready. I lifted my head . . . now we can begin. It was as I said those words that I saw him, standing tall and straight in front of me, and I laughed out loud as I saw what he held in his hand—a small silver baton. He smiled as he raised his hand, lifted the baton, and paused for just one moment, and then we began to play: he the maestro, I the musician: Grey Eagle conducting. As I followed him, my words, like music, spoken with confidence, and clearly, flowed from me.

And as I spoke, I came to the part where I mention Wendy, and remembering her, my throat threatened to close, and tears stung the back of my eyes. Struggling to remain in control I looked to Grey Eagle, knowing that this would help steady me. He was still there, still conducting, holding the baton . . . and as I spoke the words I had spoken first for Wendy, I saw her. Standing close by my guide, her eyes large and beautiful as ever, she smiled her wonderful smile for me . . . and the sun shone.

It Was
My Time

As a healer I am often called out on emergency hospital visits. This was one of those times. We'll call him Thomas, and he had been involved in an accident at work; he had been crushed by a tanker. Thomas had been rushed to the nearest hospital and had been operated on almost immediately. Three days had passed, and Thomas, now conscious, was experiencing excruciating pain, which grew worse, until his surgeon decided they should open him up again and take a second look.

Thomas was suffering severe internal bleeding and was placed on a life-support machine. His condition was slowly deteriorating. It was at this point that the RAAH was called in and I personally became involved.

Many of Thomas's friends had visited the hospital, offering help and support. One of these friends, Roy, had undergone terrible trauma himself (a car accident in which his small grandson was killed and his wife seriously injured), and on the advice of a friend he had brought his wife to one of our healing centers. For quite some time, Roy and his wife had regularly attended our healing sessions, both of them feeling that they were receiving enormous help. Roy was so impressed with my team he nicknamed us "the Love Club." Now here was his friend Thomas, desperately in need of help, and Roy told Thomas's wife, Eileen, and his children about us.

On my first visit the family was very nervous, not quite knowing what to expect. Soon we were all talking freely, they more at ease as I explained the role my team and I would play.

It is always important in circumstances such as these to be clear from the start that no miracles are promised, no cure certain. That done, I explained that my team and I would visit Thomas as often as possible, at least once a day, to give him healing and that in our own way we would do our best to help.

So now it was time to go see my patient. Quietly I walked into the intensive care unit. As always, I was unprepared for the vast array of machines, that screaming mass of human technology designed to save lives, wires and tubes around, over, and running through my patients' body, even though I had seen it many times before.

Thomas lay still on the bed. The only sound, only movement, came from the steady blip, blip, blip of the cardiac monitor. In the background uniformed nurses were quietly going about their business.

I reached forward and took Thomas's hand, and in a hushed voice I introduced myself and explained to him why I was there. There was no sign that he heard me, and as I began my work there was no response, but, unperturbed, I carried on, knowing that God was with us both.

Several days passed. My team and I had visited often, but there was no improvement. In fact, Thomas was deteriorating quite rapidly, and neither doctors or nurses could understand why he hadn't gone already.

"He's waiting," I would muse, as I stood often by his bed, looking down at him. "He's waiting, but for what?"

Then late one evening, on about the fourth day, as I stood once again by his bedside praying, from the corner of my eye I saw movement—not from Thomas, or should I say not from the form on the bed, but from the far side of the bed. I was at first so wrapped up in what I was doing that I ignored all else, assuming that Thomas's son had come to help me, as he had done before. Then, the movement was stronger, and I became aware of a male presence. I lifted my head to smile a greeting to whoever had come to keep me company.

I was not surprised when I stared up into Thomas's face, heard his voice as he introduced himself to me. My fingers tightened fractionally around his hand, but of course he would not be able to feel it. Looking to his body, lying there on the bed, then back to Thomas, Thomas in his spirit form, in his spirit body, I realized instantly that Thomas had left his physical body, had "stepped out" so that he could talk to me.

He was not dead—that silver cord, so fine, so strong, that ties us to our earth life, our earth body, was still intact, still attached, unbroken.

He spoke first, pointing to his physical form lying on the bed. "It's so heavy in there, I can't believe how light I feel," he said. "And all that pain—I think I've had enough. It feels so much better 'out.'"

"So what are you telling me?" I asked. "Have you given up, have you stopped fighting, or have you come to tell me it's your time?"

"I don't know," he said, shoulders shrugging, and pointing backward over his shoulder, he began to cry. "It's them," he said. "It's just so hard to leave them all behind."

I nodded, understanding his dilemma, understanding the dilemma of any loving parent, any loving husband. "But it's my time," I heard him whisper now, "and I truly want to go."

"How can I help?" I asked him gently. "Tell me what you need."

"Just tell them when I'm gone how much I love them, will you, Rosemary? And that I'll always be close by."

I nodded, saddened by his dilemma, and assured him I would do the best I could. Then he was gone. I looked down again at the body, not Thomas, lying on the bed, surrounded by those machines I knew to be useless to him now, even though they would keep him "alive" for two more days. I sighed, knowing that the greatest pain would be for his family, left behind.

A few months after Thomas "died," his wife, Eileen, came for a consultation, and I was, in the fullest way, able to keep my promise to him. For again I saw him, this time much more settled, and well prepared to give his wife much-needed evidence of his survival after death. And at the end of the session, as I relayed to Eileen her husband's message of love and life continuing, he smiled at me, and winking, said . . . tell her, tell her, it was my time.

As I have been writing Thomas's story, remembering the fear that he had of leaving his loved ones, remembering the fear his family experienced for him during his last days, I am reminded of a question I put to Grey Eagle, and of his answer.

Question: Grey Eagle, there are many of us who fear death. Can you give us any comfort or advice on the process of death?

Answer: There are many who fear the unknown, and what appears to be an all-embracing darkness.

You approach us with uncertainty. And, yet, all there is here is light . . . and yet all there is, is joy . . . and yet all there is, is beauty.

As each soul crosses the void which separates the two worlds, there will be a soul waiting, with hand outstretched, and joyful heart; you will be greeted and made welcome.

There will be a time of celebration. For the souls who have already gone . . . departed your earth plane . . . will know of the joy of the reunion which we have already spoken of.

No man will enter the tunnel alone. No man will step upon that path toward death without some help and guiding hand.

Always someone will whisper to you, "Look toward the light." And, you will be drawn to it. And, you will hear the chattering of excited voices. For those who await what you see as your death will be waiting and ready to celebrate your birth.

So, fear not, for death is a painless experience. The fear of leaving those behind you, who you love, will disappear . . . for you will still see them. And it will still be possible for you to be involved in their lives . . . and to watch them grow . . . and to give them aid.

Death is not a punishment.

You embark upon a new journey . . . your ticket paid . . . your passage assured . . . you will safely reach our shore . . . and no man will come alone . . . and no man's journey will be a lonely one, for there are always souls who wait for you, with joy and with happiness in their hearts, for your safe return to us.

A Different
Kind of Healing

It was Mick McGuire who brought him to me and it was so long ago I've forgotten his name, but his story is unforgettable.

Let's call him Simon. He was less than twenty years old. Mick had first met Simon after Simon had cut his wrists in an attempted suicide. He had tried several times before, failing each time to die, but succeeding in making a mess of his arms and wrists, and becoming more and more confused and desperate. He was calling out loud and clear for help.

Mick is a very fine healer, but after two or three sessions with Simon he realized that he needed a different kind of healing, one that could be given best by me. So without telling me anything of Simon's history, he asked if he could bring him along to see me.

Simon was tall and very slim, with sandy hair, very intense and extremely nervous. As I welcomed him to my home I took his hands and noticed how clammy his skin was. All Mick had told me was that this young man needed my help, and as I watched him sit, straightening himself in the chair, I knew this to be true.

At first we chatted in a light and easy way, Mick and I doing all of the talking. Simon sat stiff, tense, despite our attempts to get him to relax and join in a little. Then, Grey Eagle's voice, soft in my ear: "It's time, and we are ready for you now."

Then I saw them. A woman in her sixties, and an older woman somewhere in her late seventies or early eighties. The resemblance between them was so startling that I instantly knew them to be mother and daughter. But what I wasn't prepared for, and what I had never seen before, and indeed, have never seen since, was the way they were shoving and pushing each other.

"I want to do it," said the older one. "It's me first, he's my son, you're just his grandmother, so stop interfering," said the other. "No," and "No," and "Get out of the way."

Startled, I looked to Grey Eagle, not knowing what to do, what to make of what I was seeing.

"He's my son."

"Yes, and a fine job you did of bringing him up. Just look at him. It's your fault."

"Oh no, don't blame me, I did my best. If it wasn't for your interfering..."

And on and on they argued, squabbling like hens over a crumb of bread. Pushing, poking, shoving each other, vying for first place.

Mick and Simon were, of course, oblivious to all this, unable to see or hear, and I was careful as I talked to Grey Eagle not to let my consternation show.

"What do I do?" I whispered to my guide, puzzled because Grey Eagle, quite calm and seemingly indifferent to the wrangling and bickering, took no action to stop it.

"Why, do what you must," he said, giving me a somewhat quizzical smile. "Remember, they are guests in your home, and they need your help to talk to the boy." Then, "And remember too, Rosemary, that it is Simon who really needs help, and this is why we are all here. Don't lose sight of that fact."

While Grey Eagle and I had been talking, the two women had continued to fight. Even now as I told Simon that his mother and grandmother had come through from the spirit world to talk to him, even now, they were so engrossed in their squabbles that when I turned to them to tell them I was ready, they did not at first hear me.

Finally, after three tries, I got their attention, and asked which of them would like to talk first.

"I will," said the mother, pulling herself up to her full height. Glaring at her mother, daring her to disagree, she added, "It's my right."

Simon's grandmother stepped back, seeming to agree, and with a sigh of relief, I then asked his mother how she would like to begin.

"I want you to tell him it's not my fault," she began arrogantly, and she poked her finger at me, emphasizing each word she spoke.

Before I could comment, however, Simon's grandmother stepped in and attacked her daughter again.

"Who do you think you are," she said, "speaking to her like that?" This, pointing at me. "And it is your fault, all your fault. If you'd left him to me he wouldn't be in this state." And once again the two began to argue. And I had had enough.

"Okay" I finally yelled at them both, making myself heard over them. "This is it." Now I had their attention. "I don't know where you think you are," I continued more quietly, "but while you are here in my house there will be no more arguing. You will treat me and my home with respect, and if you can't do that, then you will leave, both of you."

As I spoke these words I gave them a look that my daughter would call "one of those looks," which meant don't fool with me. "I will not put up with this," I said. "If this is what Simon had to deal with when you were both here, it's no wonder he has problems." This last remark silenced them, for in my innocence of the situation, I had just hit the nail firmly on the head, and they knew it.

Then Simon's grandmother came forward again, more timidly now. She asked if she could tell their story, which I knew instinctively I must repeat to Simon, who so far, unaware of my conversation with his mother and grandmother, had sat patiently with Mick, waiting for me to begin. Mick had already prepared him for what I might be able to do, and so, trusting me, he had been content to wait.

Now I reached forward, reaching for Simon's hand, and gently I began to recount all that I saw and heard.

It was, as it often is, like watching a movie of someone's life, Simon's life. I saw Simon as a small boy of about three or four years old, saw him in his home, with a girl, just a little older, his sister. Then I heard arguing, not this time between his mother and grandmother, but between his mother and father. The argument was a bitter one, and I heard, rather than saw, Simon's father leave, for good, I knew.

The scene moved on a little, and I saw Simon's mother, younger then, pain and rage on her face. She was holding a framed photograph of her husband in her hands, and as I watched, she proceeded to smash it, banging the frame down again and again. The glass was broken, the frame bent. Words, filthy words, like thick bile, poured from her mouth in putrefied clots, as she defiled the name of man, of all men. With violent savagery she spewed forth this acrimony. Suddenly I was cold, so cold, and shuddered uncontrollably, for the picture grew wider. In the room, this same room, I saw the child, a small boy, gazing up at his mother, pure terror in his eyes, for it was toward him that she was venting her rage.

Recounting this, I held tightly on to Simon, knowing that he would remember all I spoke of. Mick drew close to him too, and placed his arms about the young man's shoulders, as Simon began to cry.

But there was more, and the grandmother, crying now too, continued. On past the time when Simon's father left, on through the years when Simon's mother, holding him on her knee, holding him tightly, too tightly, would call him her little boy, her precious boy, would tell him he must never leave her as his father had.

And when mentioning his father, she would again and again tell Simon that men were evil, men were wicked, men were cruel, men were filth, and more than filth, to be despised. Then she would stroke his hair, and telling him she loved him, would croon and sing, and call him her precious child.

Fights between his mother and grandmother would break out. His grandmother knew it wasn't healthy, wasn't right, but Simon's mother, so consumed by hatred, wouldn't listen. As he grew, listening to the constant arguing of the two women, listening to his mother's constant hatred of "all men," he became more and more confused. But the real problems began as he grew older, as he looked each day in the mirror, as he became a man himself. And he began to hate.

His grandmother, whom he had loved even as he had hated her, died. Then his mother died.

Still watching, still listening as Simon's grandmother continued their story, I saw him now, on his own. Grandmother gone, mother gone, his sister, married, also gone. He was not quite eighteen.

Still watching, as the "movie" rolled on, fast-forward to his mother's funeral, Simon standing by the graveside, crying, crying, crying now as I recounted what I saw.

And again the grandmother's voice, soft now, full of tears and heartache. "... and he walked away from the graveside, loving her, hating her, loving her, hating her ... and despising himself."

Mick and I sat holding Simon, the only sound in the room his quiet sobbing. And his tears flowed.

"Should I go on?" I asked of Grey Eagle, and he replied, "Yes, child, you must."

I shifted in my chair and brought my attention back to the two women. Simon's mother stood quietly now, also crying. His grandmother, relieved to finally be able to talk, nodded that she was ready to go on.

The scene moved before my eyes, and this time Simon was in the bathroom, standing in front of the mirror.

"I hate you, I hate you," and he began beating his fists against the glass, as he had done many times before. "You're nothing but a man . . . a disgusting, filthy man . . . a disgusting, filthy man . . ." Then, sobbing, "And she hated you too . . . she hated you too." For a moment longer he stared, wild-eyed, into the mirror, then, as I watched, he took up the razor blade and began to cut. Blood ran, tears ran . . . and screams ran, screams and screams and screams ran from his mouth. All those screams, for all those years that he had held them in his head. And then he fell.

And then again, and then again, and each time, as he tried to kill the vile man he knew himself to be, I saw it. And his grandmother saw. And his mother saw.

And then I heard her voice, not quite a whisper, and full of tears, as she stepped forward. Her head bowed, her shoulders slumped. "I did, I did it. It was all my fault, my doing," and she cried and cried. Simon's grandmother, turning, seeing her daughter's final realization, moved toward her, and placing her arms around her, crying too, said quietly, "No, dear, no, we both did it, we are both to blame."

I had continued, through all of this, to recount all to Simon and to Mick. Now, just as his mother had gone into his grandmother's arms, so now Simon came into mine.

It was an hour or two later when Simon and Mick left my house. We had talked for a long time about his mother, her life and her confusions, and Simon had begun to realize that the real problem lay not with him but with her. She was the one who had been ugly and hateful, not he. He began, too, to realize that it was her bitterness toward his father that had turned her this way. And Mick and I helped him see that although she had been these things, she did love him very much.

From that day, Simon began to heal. It was a lengthy process, for no one can expect that years and years of damage can be healed in an instant.

As he was Mick's patient, I didn't see Simon again until about eighteen months later. I was giving a lecture in Doncaster, Mick was coming with me, and we had arranged to meet in the parking lot of the place we were speaking at. Mick's car pulled up at the same moment I arrived, and, waving, I climbed out of my car. As I bent to lock the door I heard a voice, and I turned and watched as a young man bounded across the parking lot toward me.

"Rosemary, Rosemary," he called. It was only as he swept me up in a big hug that I realized who he was. Not the Simon that I remembered, but this young man, tanned, smiling, healthy, looking down at me now with tears in his eyes, tears of joy at our reunion. This Simon, I knew, was well on his way to being healed.

His mother? His grandmother? What of them? To be honest with you, I do not know. My hope is that they too have chosen to have healing, that they too wish to face and to deal with . . . themselves, with who they were, how they were, how they affected others in their lives here on this earth. And if they have chosen that path, then they too will be helped, and will, in time, be healed also.

We often forget, in the structural society that we live in today, how much parents' words have impact on their, our, children, how potentially dangerous our words can be. Simon's is a horror story. That it has a happy ending makes it no less so.

As a parent, looking back on the last twenty-six years of my child's life, I know I have done many things, said many things, that have not been good. Please God I did no great harm. Please God, who gave this child to my care, that I taught her not only to love me, to love others, but that I taught her to love herself. For she is beautiful, as all our children are . . . as Simon is . . .

I'm Picking
Daisies

I was in America. It was May 11, the day before Mother's Day. I was speaking to a small group, seven families, mothers, fathers, and siblings of seven boys who had died.

We were in Nashua, New Hampshire, a town I had never visited before. The only reason I was there, for my time on this particular trip was very limited, was that children are my priority, and I knew that they needed my voice.

It is very hard, especially with a small group, to explain that I can promise nothing, that there are no guarantees that I will be able to make contact with the spirit world. I hear myself say it, knowing it to be true. I see my audience nod in understanding, accepting what I say. But I see their eyes, hopeful, desperate, and I know that I cannot in any way protect them from the disappointment they will experience if I fail to connect.

But it is worth the risk, worth the hurt, for if we do not try, then how will we know if we can succeed? And so, trusting the will of heaven, God's will, then I begin.

And this time it begins to work, and as I proceed, the tension in the room begins to lift, and all there become more relaxed. It's working—yes, it's working after all.

As I sit talking to them, slowly, slowly, I see their boys, and my hand gently caresses the roses, seven small roses, that were given me by this group before I began. Seven roses, seven sweet flowers, each representing a child of the spirit world. And flowers are appropriate that day.

First one, then another and another, the boys begin to talk to me.

"I closed my eyes and slipped away, and when they came to wake me I was gone," said one. His parents nodded, mother and sister accepting, father doubtful, until his boy gave more evidence that he was alive.

"I saw him fixing the faucet," said another, pointing to his dad after he had told me how he had died in an accident. "He tried to take a short cut, but it didn't work, and he had to take them off again and clean the pipe." Another father shook his head, not disbelieving but finding it difficult to comprehend the accuracy of a message he had been given.

"He's wearing my hat," another boy boldly announced, and there was much laughter then, as the father admitted this was true. "And my watch," his son continued, giving me a cheeky grin, "and tell him I know it keeps losing time." It does too, his father burst out, it was ten minutes slow this morning. "My mom is wearing her chain, her special chain, too," the boy continued, and his mother gasped in delight as she pulled the chain out from under her sweater.

"My father sells shoes, they are fixing up the house, I see them, I see them," says a young teenager who was killed by a drunk driver. He proceeds to give messages to his brother and sister, as all the boys do.

On and on it went, as each of the seven boys gave evidence of his survival after death. I watched and listened, gave messages that united, reunited, these families, watched, listened, as they laughed and they cried, and I saw healing, great healing, taking place.

I had been working now for about three hours, giving much

more detail and evidence than I have space to document in this book. I had been working solidly, without a break. I knew I could not go on much longer, for I could feel energy draining from me, but I could not stop yet, as one more family remained.

A husband and wife, no children, no children present . . . except, of course, one son.

This boy was different from the others. He was desperate to make contact with his parents, like the others, and was emotional, hesitant, wanting to do his best, also like the others. But the other six boys had had no control over how they had "died." This boy had had control.

"It was my fault, my doing," he began. "The car, the car."

Hearing him talk of the car I could easily have assumed a road accident. However, the more he talked to me the more I realized that this boy had died by his own hand. He had sat in the car while he was shooting heroin into himself. The problem his parents had was that they, the father in particular, blamed themselves.

I heard his voice again. "An investigation. Police, police. Questions. They asked questions. It was all my fault. Please tell my dad, my mom, it was me, I did it to myself."

Both parents broke down, the father sobbing almost uncontrollably at first. Then as if the boy knew that his message was fully understood, he began to relax and was able to show his parents that he was okay, that he was alive and well, and above all, safe. Soon everyone in the room was smiling, all still grieving, but happy in the knowledge that their children had survived death.

And there was a final message from the seven boys, and it was a message that no one there could understand but me.

"Tell them," they called to me with one voice, "tell them we're helping to pick daisies."

I was in England, and it must have been around 1990 or 1991—the exact date escapes me. Only the story remains imprinted in my head, as it was the first time, other than with my students, that I was to do this.

The couple sitting opposite me in my small study had lost their son. He had been killed in a road accident just prior to his twenty-first birthday. I had spoken to Richard many times, given messages often to his parents, and here they were once again, needing and asking for my help.

Mary, Richard's mother, spoke first. "It's Bill," she said, indicating her husband, Richard's father. "He's becoming more and more depressed as time goes by. It's ten years now since we lost Richard, and instead of getting better, Bill just seems to be getting worse, and I don't know what to do anymore." She finished this last comment on a sob, and I looked to where Bill sat, tears streaming down his face, nodding in agreement with his wife.

"So what is it you want, Bill?" I asked, knowing that his answer would be "My son," knowing and saying, "I cannot bring him back to you, except through the usual channels. Richard has given you so much evidence over the years of his survival after death. What more can I do?"

"I only want to see him, to know that he's safe," replied Bill, unashamed of the tears he was shedding. "Just to know, to see, what he's doing, how he's spending his time."

For a while longer we talked. Bill was a patient as well as a client and had received healing many times over the years from me and my team, at one of our healing centers. It was as I asked if his healing had helped him at all that I heard Grey Eagle's voice.

"We will take him on a journey, and he can visit with his son. Take his hand and help him cross the void which separates our worlds."

I listened further. "Hold his hand, little one. I will help you help him." Looking toward Bill, I saw Richard standing beside him, smiling slightly, waiting.

With my students, I mused, it is part of their training—to enable them, through many years of dedicated schooling, to raise their level of consciousness to the point where they can free themselves of their physical body, free themselves to travel, to explore, to meet with others in the spirit world. This is not an easy task, and can take years to learn, and many of my students never make it past the first two or three stages.

I looked again at Bill, heard Grey Eagle's voice, sure and encouraging, saw Richard, who, obviously prepared, knowing this would be, patiently waited for me to begin.

"How would you like to go with me?" I began, gently reaching for Bill's hand, then explaining that it might be possible for him to see, to experience, his son in a somewhat unusual but nevertheless very real way. I told him a little about the process, how it would feel to him at first very much like experiencing healing, but we would go further, deeper, that we would travel. His reaction was not one of surprise or doubt, as one might expect with such a seemingly outlandish proposition. Instead, he just squeezed my hand a little tighter. "I had a dream," he said, "a very vivid dream, that I was with Richard, that we were flying. Maybe," he said hesitantly, "it wasn't a dream after all. Maybe I was just being prepared."

For the first time since he had walked into my study, Bill smiled. Then, nodding his head, he said, "I'm ready. Tell me what to do. I'm right with you."

And so we began. As always prior to healing of any kind—and this was surely a healing experience—I said a prayer, asking God's protection, his help and guidance, and for the best results for my patient. Then, placing my hands in his, slowly I raised my level of conscious thought, and giving my energy, my mind power, to Bill, I began to talk.

"Richard is here." As I said this I moved back into my own chair. "He is reaching out to you."

I heard Bill gasp, lift his hand, and squeeze. Bill's wife, sitting quietly, trusting, could only see her husband, could not see as Richard placed his hand in his dad's hand and lifted him up.

Mary could see her husband, his physical body, but could not see, as I could, Bill's etheric body pull away from the physical to join his son.

I watched, and now it was like a vision, for it seemed as if I were looking at a movie screen. They were like two Peter Pans, flying, floating, as in a fairy tale.

They were inside a church, and I watched as they held each other. I noticed the window, high up, behind the altar, large and round, beautiful stained glass, the sun shining through it, making the colors glow bright.

"We'll go out through the window," I heard the boy say to his father. "Don't panic, Dad, you're with me now. Just hang on."

Quietly I spoke, more to Mary now than to her husband, describing all that I was seeing and hearing. To Mary's eyes, Bill was asleep, and only the telltale tears rolling down his cheeks told her something more was going on.

They passed through the glass as if it were not there, and flew, floated, out, up, into the sun. The sky was blue, such healing blue, then dark, then stars, then blue again.

Still I watched, part of the scene, not intruding on their togetherness, but with them just the same.

The sun was shining in a bright and clear blue sky. Still flying, now they were passing over rolling green hills. Then, "We're going down now, Dad, into the valley, see?" And they floated down over fields so green and lush, the beauty took my breath away. On and on, time racing on, but oh so slowly, we came at last to Richard's field. Waving his hand out over this meadow of green, green grass and daisies, white-petaled with yellow-gold centers, so many daisies, Richard turned again and spoke to his father.

"When I was with you on the earth plane I became a nurse. I cared for the sick, for those in pain who could not care for themselves. My need for growth, my soul's need, was great, and through my work I learned many things about myself. I am a carer, I am a light that needs to grow, will grow, as I continue to care, to give, to help."

He waved his hand about him, indicating again the field of daisies. I saw, felt, a cool breeze as it wafted through the field. Saw the daisies, their heads lifted full up to the sun, saw them sway softly, dance in the sunlight.

"This is the field where daisies grow. When you look, all you see are flowers. When she looks"—and I heard, and knew that he meant me—"when she looks, she sees what we see. For each perfect and beautiful flower is a child. Each perfect blossom, lifting its face upward toward the sun, toward the light, each tiny daisy, is a small child, getting ready to come to us.

"Before a child comes to us we know, we know of their coming. We must be ready, ready to help them, ready to carry them to the light. And angels come, and always, angels come. Very gently, so very carefully, we lift each flower, and as its roots come away from the earth, then we help the angels carry them to a good place, to God.

"I am still a carer, Dad. It's what I want to do. There are many of us here, kids like me, who help the children when they come, we help the angels in their work."

Turning now, he smiled the brightest smile. "It's time for me to take you back now, Dad," and Bill nodded, returning his son's smile. Again I watched as they flew, floated, over fields, mountains, through the sun, into the dark, into a star-lit sky, and down, and down, and down . . . and back.

Bill stirred in his chair, and as I watched him I knew that a great healing had taken place, that Bill had had his "journey toward healing."

For one moment I thought it was over. Then I saw Bill's hand, still clasped tight, holding Richard's hand. Heard Richard's voice, closer now, and I knew that Bill still heard, that some small part of him was with Richard still. And so I waited. Then I heard,

"It's time now, Dad, time for me to leave. I love you, Dad, I love you. Now you know where I am, and what I do, and we are both more at peace. So don't think I'm idle, that there is nothing to do. I'm just as busy as ever, helping to ensure there are no lost souls.

"And Dad, if anyone asks, if anyone wants to know"—and at this he laughed, the most joyous sound—"Just tell them . . . I'm picking daisies."

And God,
and Christ,
and Spirit Guides

What I am about to tell you now will, I know, make me sound like a religious fanatic, or a crazy person, or perhaps even a charlatan. I don't believe that I am any of these. As I say this I am reminded of all those people in the past who have claimed to see the Virgin Mary or Christ, people who have claimed that, as in a vision, some saint has come to them to give them a message meant for mankind. The children of Fatima, Bernadette of Lourdes, Joan of Arc, these and many more have told of their visions.

I don't claim that my vision was for mankind. I do claim that I had a vision, but that vision was for me and not, I feel, for anyone else.

It was on a night when my friends and healers, Mick McGuire, Brian Boyle, Adele Campion, and Paul Denham, were with me at my house. Mick, I remember, was over at the far side of the room with Paul and Brian, giving healing to Adele, who had had a particularly stressful day. I sat on the sofa at the other end of the room, watching, helping in my own small way, sending out a prayer to God, to Christ, that healing could be given.

This was in the early days, less than a year after my initial meeting with the Denhams, who were among the first to recognize my abilities as a medium. Healing was new to me then. Mick was the healer, not I, not in any way, not I. Nor did I want to be. Sickness scared me, I found hospitals daunting, and if anyone had told me, before this night, that I would become a healer, would found a healing organization, I would have laughed in disbelief. Not me, not me—I was not that good . . . and I was too scared.

But I was happy to help. If all that was expected of me was that I pray, I could do that. That part was easy. After all, Christ was my friend. I had known him all my life, had worshiped him, revered him, respected and loved him for as long as I could remember. And besides, he was my salvation.

"The Lord is my shepherd."

And he is, I felt, and still feel. He truly is.

So I sat this night on the sofa and prayed.

I don't remember how long I prayed. I could tell you it was but a moment, yet it could have been thirty minutes. The room was softly lit and quiet, and I was aware of Mick and Paul and Brian standing around Adele, with their hands on her head and shoulders, also praying. And I was aware too of a great peace which had settled over us.

I looked up, looked away from the others, down the length of the room, where my old rocking chair stood, and it was there I saw him. I stared, not believing, shook my head, and turned away, squeezed my eyes tight shut. "I'm tired," I thought. "I haven't been sleeping well." Then I turned and looked back to the rocking chair.

It was not a dream, not even a vision, but a stark reality, and I knew as I looked into his eyes, though no words had yet been spoken, that I was looking at Christ.

He stood quietly by the side of the rocking chair, his arms outstretched to me. The words "Suffer little children" went through my head.

"Are you real?" I whispered quietly. His smile as I asked this, the light that shone around him and the look of purity and love in his eyes, gave me my answer.

For a moment longer, which seemed like an eternity, I gazed on him, and all the love I had ever felt in my life I felt for him. Then, turning, wanting to share this moment with my friends, I saw them watching me. They had finished their healing session, and were now looking at me, inscrutable expressions on their faces.

"Do you see him?" I whispered again, tentatively, not wanting to break the spell or destroy the moment. As I spoke I could taste the salty tears which had rained silently down my cheeks.

In unison they shook their heads, they too aware of magic in the air. Then Mick, his throat dry, whispered hoarsely back, "See *who*, Rosemary? See *who?*"

I turned back to where my Savior had been standing just moments before, and he was gone. But the space where He had been was filled with light, and I knew with greater certainty than I had ever felt in my life before that the Lord was truly my shepherd.

It was several months before I became seriously involved with what is referred to as "spiritual healing." Since that time I have had many patients. And there have been those times, not often, not often enough, when I have laid my hands gently on a patient's shoulders as I said my healing prayer, and I have seen Christ's hands, placed just as gently over mine, have felt their gentle pressure, and experienced such a warmth and love and light pass through me.

As I have traveled around the world I have been asked by many people this question: How can you believe in Christ and yet say that you have a spirit guide, an Apache no less, who is your teacher, your mentor? So many people assume that to believe in Christ is to exempt all other helpers. For me this is not so. I believe that God has many helpers, many messengers. Christ, angels, spirit guides . . . all doing the work they are supposed to do, all helping one another, working alongside one another. Each equally important in God's eyes, even as we who are of the earth are each of us equal in God's eyes. Christ taught us that. And so I work with Grey Eagle, a man of God, working in God's name, knowing that Christ is leading us forward.

As there is much connected to God and to the universe that we don't understand, so too there are many different ways to give healing. The story I am going to tell now is one that defies understanding. So it must, if I am to tell it, be understood at least that I cannot provide an explanation of how this was. I can only tell you that it was.

Angie was a young woman. Sexually and physically abused by her father from the age of eight, at sixteen she ran away from home. She ended up in a psychiatric ward in a hospital in the small town of Scunthorpe in the north of England, where finally her father's constant abuse was discovered. Since then she had met and fallen in love with a young man, the father of her only child, a daughter, Leah. This relationship, doomed from the beginning, broke up when the child was but a few months old, and soon after she met the man she would love and marry.

Only a short time after she married, tragedy struck again: she was diagnosed as having a rare and terminal illness. Her lungs were diseased, and there was no cure.

Angie had been in a hospital for several months and had had one of her lungs removed, and although her husband had visited regularly at first, as the weeks went by his visits tapered to nothing. Hurt, afraid, confused, when she was eventually allowed out of the hospital she returned home, thinking she would be returning to her husband and child. She was met at the door by a young woman who claimed to be her husband's common-law wife. His wife, she explained, had committed suicide, leaving their small daughter in the care of her father.

Shocked, numb, Angie raced into the house, hardly able to breathe, still weak from her operation. She picked up her sleeping child and left.

Several years passed—several years of sickness, of pain, as she became steadily worse, as she had been told she would.

Leah grew, used to seeing her mother sick, used to the times when her mother would be rushed to the hospital, used to being told, "Your mother is dying," knowing the inevitable, learning to live with it, but still, in those times when her mother took turns for the worse, afraid.

When Angie first came to me, to one of our healing centers, she had been given less than five years to live. Her one remaining lung was slowly filling with diseased mucus, taking her life's breath, drowning her. Her heart too had become enlarged, damaged, with the effort of breathing.

Over the eight-year period that she has been my patient—yes, we are ahead by three years so far—I have been with Angie through some of her many ordeals. I have heard her doctors say many times, "She can't survive this one. This time it really is the end." And each time, so close to death, a miracle has happened, and she has pulled through.

The knowledge that her daughter, Leah, now fifteen, needs her is her strength. Her fight for life is not for herself, but for her child. She knows, too, that the healing she has received has been a gift to her, God's gift to her, for without it she feels she would not have been able to go on for so long. Hers is a true courage, true bravery, for she has had no support from her family, and apart from a few good friends she has had to stand alone.

Perhaps two years prior to the time of my writing this, on returning to England from America, I was called to Angie's bedside. It was an emergency. This time she would not survive. It was impossible, she was much too sick.

An October day, it was the day my mother died. One of my sisters had called to say that my mother had passed early that morning. It was also the day that Angie's father died, later in the morning.

I arrived at Angie's bedside at about three in the afternoon. She was just holding on, waiting for me to come. As I sat down next to her I noticed how small and frail she had become. She was only thirty-two, but lying there she looked like an old woman. An oxygen mask was strapped to her face, and her breathing was irregular. She clung to my hand.

"I'm afraid," she said, and tears trickled from her eyes. "I don't want to meet *him*." I knew, of course, that she was referring to her father, and I began to reassure her that he would not be around. "And anyway," I said, "what makes you think you're going anywhere? You are not going to die just yet, you know."

I said this last with such conviction, believing it myself, that Angie smiled. It was a small, trembling smile, a smile which asked the question "Do you really mean that?"—at the same time trusting that I did.

We sat quietly for a while, I, still holding her hand, giving her healing. Suddenly she turned and looked me square in the eye.

"Will you take me on a journey?" she asked. "I know you can, I've heard you say so. Will you take me traveling?"

It was as if her soul knew her needs, was voicing those needs, and my soul answered in reply, knowing too that it was right.

Up, up, up we soared, I out of my body, Angie out of hers. Grey Eagle was with us, and as we rose up toward him he seemed to turn into a large bird, an eagle. Slowly, carefully, I helped Angie, and we climbed on to the eagle's back.

At first his wings flapped softly, then with more force. I felt the wind from them on my face, felt my hair blow back. Angie felt it too, and we began to rise, higher and higher, traveling through blue clouds, bright sunshine, breathing pure, clean air. And then we began to laugh, softly at first, then louder as we experienced the real meaning of the phrase "Let your spirit soar," and we went higher, and higher still, and were set free as we moved into the light.

Our journey took less than an hour, more than a lifetime, and when I left Angie she was in a deep and healing sleep. I wondered vaguely how much she would remember, knowing that her soul would always keep the memory.

When I left her, Angie's friends still thought that Angie's life was over. I smiled at them, knowing this was not the way it was to be, telling them I would be back later that evening.

The next morning, she fully came out of the crisis, and when I arrived she was sitting up eating breakfast and looking much better.

As I said at the beginning, I cannot tell you the hows and whys of this healing experience, I can only say that it happened, and that it worked.

Part IV

CASEBOOK
REVISITED

I HAVE, AS I HAVE SAID MANY TIMES BEFORE, NEVER CLAIMED TO be a writer, merely a teller of stories, true stories. Stories which I hope will provide us all with so many insights, so much knowledge, so much teaching. The casebook section in *The Eagle and the Rose* was so well received that it needs no more from me than to begin, as all good storytellers begin, "Once upon a time..."

Auras

This is a story I love, which was told to me many years ago. It is about an elderly lady who was a regular churchgoer in a rather quaint village, the congregation much the same week after week. Over the years many ministers had come and gone. The old lady had "her" seat, the same one each week, and her routine was always the same. Rarely did she speak to anyone, afraid perhaps of seeming forward, but she always attended meetings, fêtes, and all the other churchly activities, and by her presence was supportive.

The other members of the church, although never unkind, rarely, if ever, consulted the old woman or involved her in any of the decision-making. And so it was not at all surprising that when the new minister arrived, she was the last to know.

He was young and charming and seemed to bring new life to the church. Everyone took to him, and the church blossomed. Until, that is, he disappeared. Some nine or ten months after he arrived, he simply packed up his belongings and moved on without a word to anyone.

A week or two later it was discovered that the church funds had disappeared too.

A meeting of all church members was held, and there was a lot of discussion about how everyone had been so easily fooled. The common cry was, "We all thought he was such a good man, a man of God."

It was then, after so many years of saying so little, that the old lady spoke up.

"But I thought you all knew," she said. "After all, surely you could see he wasn't a minister. He didn't have a golden light around him like the others did."

Is it an accident that the painting *The Light of the World* by William Holman Hunt shows Christ with the light behind him, or that *The Ascension of Christ* by Rembrandt and many other paintings by religious artists, great painters of holy pictures, all depict saints and godly men and women with a golden aura? I don't think so. More probable, I feel, is that these artists, involved as they were in their craft, became so close to their subjects, their sensitivities so heightened, that it was possible for them to become attuned to the power and energy of their subject and therefore to see, to visualize in some way, their aura—or God energy—and to paint it. Most, if not all, of us are born, I believe, with the ability to "see" or to sense auras. Many would agree but suggest that this is perhaps for most a lost art. I am more optimistic, believing that this art is not lost, merely mislaid, and that if we search in the right way it is more than possible to rediscover it.

Every living thing has an aura, an energy field—every plant, every tree, every insect, fish, fowl, all that breathes, including humans, of course.

Since I can remember, I have been aware of color and shade around people. Not knowing that I was seeing energy, and not realizing that others could not see, I never took much notice. For me, it was natural, but not especially well developed. I pushed it away. It was too confusing and simply added to the terror that was my life as I was growing up.

It was only after I met Grey Eagle that I became more curious about auras and began to make more conscious efforts to "aura-spot." And after a discussion we had about flying insects, which the American Indians call "the tiny winged people," I became somewhat intrigued by the auras of insects, beetles, spiders, and the like.

I remember watching TV one evening when something caught my eye. I turned, and there crawling on the wall next to me was a wood louse. But what fascinated me was the tiny pinprick of light which followed it, like a shadow. As this insect crawled up and down, the light hovered over and around it. Its aura was pure and uncluttered, very different from a human aura, which has many colors, many shades.

I also remember the first time I saw a spider's aura. It was just the same, an intense bright light, like a spotlight, moving as the spider moved, pure and bright and uncluttered.

A friend once asked, a little ruefully, as she stepped on an ant, "Rosemary, what happens to it now? Does it go to the spirit world?"

Even as she asked the question I heard and repeated Grey Eagle's answer: "It becomes light."

Each living thing, great or small, has an aura. Every aura is simply energy. That energy, God energy, shows itself in many ways, and can be used, constructively and creatively, to enhance our lives.

Our aura, our energy field, is full of color, pure light, which emanates from us, expanding sometimes several feet around us. Who we are, what we are, how healthy we are—all of these things, all our emotions, are reflected in this energy. As we grow and learn, as we become more spiritual, our aura becomes considerably brighter. If there is within us a need to develop our sense of spirit, of God, and if we recognize that need, then this too reflects in our aura, which then becomes more and more full of light. And like a beacon, this light shines out into the universe, and is seen and recognized by God, by the universe. And those in the spirit world, encouraged by our spiritual growth, will draw close to us, and closer still.

And
Through Their Son

They were ordinary, hardworking, middle-class people. She was a senior district nurse in her forties. He, also in his forties, had lived in the small town of Thorne, North Yorkshire, for most of his life and worked for the local council.

Lynn Boulton was short, a little on the plump side, with dark curly hair and bright intelligent eyes, which would, I suspected, be quick to light up with laughter. But there was no trace of a smile there now as she sat with her husband, Peter, waiting for me to begin. He, around five feet eight, with light brown hair tending toward thinning, sat stiff and unbending, his suspicions about my abilities plain in the set of his jaw and the stubborn look on his face.

Although this was our first meeting, I had actually encountered the Boultons several weeks earlier. I had been speaking to a group of around three hundred people, demonstrating my gift, and had given many messages to my audience from those in the spirit world. Everything was going well. As always there was a great deal of emotion displayed as, one after the other, my communicators from the spirit world had given evidence to their loved ones of their survival after death.

It was as the evening was drawing to a close that I heard him, his voice urgent and insisting, calling out to me. "Stephen, I want to talk to Stephen. He's at the back, go to the back. Please . . . I want Stephen, I want to talk to Stephen."

Tentatively, I reached out to my audience. "I'm somewhere at the back of the hall," I said, frustrated that I couldn't quite place where I needed to be. I knew instinctively that "he," my communicator, was trying to reach someone seated to my right, and probably in the last two or three rows, but my audience was so arranged that it was impossible for me to pinpoint exactly where. Again I heard his voice, this time so clear that I was able to define that this was a young man I was hearing, and I asked him to give me a little information about himself.

"It was an accident, I was killed in an accident." Then, "Please . . . Stephen . . . Stephen . . . I need to talk to Stephen."

Now feeling more confident, I addressed my patient audience. "I'm somewhere in the back three rows, to the right. I'm hearing a young man who died in an accident calling out for Stephen. Is there a Stephen at the back there?"

No response. Plenty of people turned their heads, looking, waiting, but no Stephen.

I tried once more, repeating what I had just said, and at the same time asking the young man who stood at my side to give me more information.

But yet again, and aware of his frustration, I heard him call the name Stephen.

I went back to my audience, telling them I understood how difficult it was when, perhaps unexpectedly, they found themselves singled out, afraid and nervous about how to react. It was easy not to react at all. "But I have a young man here," I said, "who has a need to give a message to Stephen. He wants nothing more than to tell Stephen that he is alive. That he has survived death and is safe."

As I was saying these words I saw a hand go up at the back of the hall, and a woman called out, "Stephen's here with me."

"Can I see him?" I asked. "Will he please stand up?"

There was some conferring, and then I saw two heads: a woman, short and slim, and a blond-haired boy of about thirteen.

"This is Stephen," she said, "and I'm his aunt."

Now I was faced with a small problem. I knew that this was the boy I had been seeking—I could hear the young man next to me, now excited, saying, "He's my brother, he's my brother." But what to do about it? I had a rule. I never talk to children under the age of eighteen without their parents present. To do otherwise is, I consider, just too irresponsible, and so I explained this to Stephen's aunt and prepared, reluctantly, to move on.

"Wait a moment," she called. I watched as there was more conferring, then she said, "Stephen's parents are here. They don't want to stand up, but they say it's okay for you to continue." With that I saw two more hands go up, and a man's voice told me to go on.

I felt a hand on my shoulder, and I turned to Stephen's brother. He began to explain to me how he had died.

"I was on my bike," he said. "It was very sudden."

I repeated this, and Stephen's aunt confirmed that, yes, Stephen's brother had been killed in an accident while on his bike, that it was sudden and, obviously, unexpected. All the time she was saying this I was aware of my audience. It was a small town I was in, and lots of people knew one another. Many were nodding, having heard of this tragedy. And, too, I was listening to Stephen's brother give his message to me, his message to his family and to the brother he loved so much.

As I gave this message the atmosphere was electric, because so many people understood the situation. Even though I was a little confused by the last part of the message, I knew there would be many, not just Stephen and his family, who would go home that night more hopeful, reassured that their loved ones had survived death.

"The young man I have standing beside me is calling out to his brother, Stephen. I hear him say he loves you, that you have cried so much, that there has been so much pain with his passing. He talks to me of the accident, how he was on his bike when he was hit. I hear him call out to his mother, to his father, that he loves them, that he is safe. And I hear him call out to Stephen, too, that he loves him and is often with him. Then I hear him say a strange thing. I hear him say, 'Tell them not to worry. . . . I've got all my parts back, all my bits and pieces, and I am whole again.'"

Once more I was aware of my audience. There was silence in the hall, broken only by the sobbing of those who knew the story of Stephen and his brother, and who were moved by his message.

And now here I was, several weeks later, sitting with Stephen's parents in my study in the hope that we could again communicate with their son, Nigel, which, thank God, we were able to do.

When Nigel told his story, giving more and more evidence of his survival, I learned the significance of the last part of the message he had given those few weeks before. Nigel, sixteen years old, was out riding on his new moped when he had to cross an unmarked railroad crossing. There was no signal, no warning. The train hit him and carried his body several yards down the track. It was days before all of Nigel's body was found, "in pieces," and this had been a source of immense pain to Nigel's family. No wonder, then, that this young man had been so insistent on making it plain to his family that, in his own words, "I am whole again."

But the story doesn't end there. And there is a reason why I chose this story to tell among so many equally tragic, equally traumatic. This is the story of the Boultons—Peter, Lynn, Nigel, and Stephen, who, after so many years of knowing them, I count among my closest friends.

I began by describing the Boultons as "ordinary people." They had never been particularly interested in things spiritual, had never seriously questioned God, the universe, or their place in it. Their lives had been centered on their children, their work, their families. And if anyone had asked them the question "Do you believe that there are people who can talk to spirits?" they would have dismissed the idea as nonsense. Lynn and Peter are definitely the no-nonsense kind. Peter was brought up on fairgrounds. His was a tough childhood, and he was thirteen years old before his parents settled down in the mining town of Thorne. Lynn, an only child, had spent her life in this same town and had trained as a nurse, and she and Peter had married in their early twenties.

Their spiritual journey began when Nigel was killed. That was when they seriously began to question the point of their existence, and the existence of God.

It was shortly before I met them that my students and I had begun our first healing clinic, and not long afterward the Boulton family paid us their first visit. In need of healing, and wanting, too, to learn more about the spiritual aspect of their lives, they eventually became my students.

At each class they were given exercises, as were all my students. They found their training was not easy, and over the years there were many times they almost gave up, doubtful of their ability to learn. The hardest part of their learning, as for all my students, was learning about themselves. But they discovered, through exercises, that the key is to know yourself, to really be able to communicate with yourself and to learn to trust your "instincts." You must do that before you can "instinctively" attune to that power, that energy, which is of God and the universe.

In my next book, *You Own the Power*, I will talk more about instincts and attunement. Although the exercises in this book are not designed to enable you to become a healer, they are for you, about you, who you are, why you are, how you are—your sensitivity, your own spiritual power. So it is with my students in my healing organization, the RAAH. Many of the exercises they do and much of their learning is centered on self-discovery. I can remember, quite distinctly, Lynn Boulton's reaction when she first attempted an exercise, the art of relaxation, which requires us to give loving and gentle thoughts to our physical body. This can be hard, as there are not too many of us, I think, who are totally pleased with the way God made us. Too fat, too thin, too short or tall . . . we all have some complaint. With Lynn it was her legs. She hated them, always had. The shape of them, if she thought too hard, repulsed her. When she was younger she had longed to be slimmer, shapelier . . . in her eyes, more perfect.

Now she was in a room with her fellow students, required not only to examine herself physically, but to concentrate on every inch, every fiber of her being, in a caring and nonjudgmental way. If it had been one of her patients, perhaps crippled or deformed and ugly-looking, she would have found it easy—indeed she had, again and again in her profession, reached out with gentleness to bathe an ulcerated leg, massage a broken body. Her ability, driven by her compassion, to see the physical, give ease to the physical, and then look beyond to see the person is such that she can reach out with a loving hand, and with no thought, give love.

So why, when looking at herself, could she feel only disgust? Why was her judgment of herself so harsh, so uncompromising, so without love? And why is it that way with so many of us? Perhaps not all of us feel disgust, but certainly we feel some dissatisfaction.

Perhaps we have never been taught to give to ourselves. Perhaps we have been taught that to love ourselves is vanity . . . to give to ourselves is selfish . . . to like ourselves is audacious. But as a teacher, perhaps as your teacher, I have a duty to say, to teach, that as we learn to like ourselves it is because we have dared to become better human beings. To learn to give to ourselves is to understand the need of the self for self-respect. And to learn to love ourselves is to come to the awakening, the realization, of the fact that we, each individual, is of God, part of God, and of his light. And how can we not love God? And how can we not give to God? And how can we not like God, and the light which is God?

Be careful here to understand. I am not saying that each of us is God, only that all of us have God within, and if we deny ourselves love, we deny God. And so it was that Lynn and Peter Boulton began their journey of self-healing and spiritual awakening. A hard but fulfilling task.

Nothing of what I say here changes the fact that their eldest son was killed. The fact that they have become healers does not exempt them from the pain they feel every day of their lives because of his loss.

They are my friends. I count myself lucky to have such friends as these. And because I am their friend, and because I have watched them, in my own way cared for them, prayed for them, and for Stephen, who is still with us, and for Nigel, who is also still with us, albeit in another way, because I am their friend, I can truly say that through their son they have found God . . . and through their son they have found some measure of peace . . . and through their son they have found light . . . and last, yes . . . and through their son they have found themselves.

High in
the Sky

I'm not sure of the time of year, only that it was 1989 and I was coming back from a trip to Hong Kong. Back to England, I mean, home at that time, home, in the north, north of Lincolnshire.

Prior to my visit, Samantha, now aged nineteen, had been stuck. Having just completed a three-year beauty therapy course, finding herself in a part of the country where jobs were scarce, and at a time of serious economic recession, she had been at a loss as to how to proceed.

It seemed to me the perfect time to take her traveling.

"How about coming with me to Hong Kong?" I asked. I had planned to stay for four months. "You could get a job out there, work behind a bar, or maybe in a beautician's, waitressing, doesn't matter what, and have some fun, experience the Far East."

Samantha agreed. It was that simple, and she had found a job at the Hong Kong Hilton, had made lots of friends, was having a ball, and had decided to stay for a while.

I, however, had to return home. Leaving my child, even though she was, of course, no longer a child, and even though my many friends in Hong Kong had promised to watch out for her, leaving

167

her was difficult for me. As I boarded the plane I was struggling with my emotions.

My seat was on the aisle in a row of three. An older woman sat in the seat nearest the window, and the middle seat was taken by a man in his early forties, tall, slim, and quite good-looking. The two of them were traveling together. As she explained to me later, although they were not related they were like mother and son.

They were very friendly, and it was obvious to me that they wanted to chat. I smiled as they introduced themselves and I gave them my name, secretly hoping they wouldn't be too friendly, too talkative. On a long flight like this one, some fourteen hours, it is always nice to meet new people—it helps the time pass. But I have had one or two bad experiences. One time I remember sitting next to a man who, obviously ill and smelling dreadfully, constantly complained that he was going to be sick. (I stood it for about an hour before insisting to the stewardess that I be moved.) Another time, it was an Arab gentleman who showed me photographs of his wife and four small children, then proceeded to proposition me on and off, for almost the entire flight. So I was a little wary of being too friendly.

However, as it turned out they were really very nice. I don't remember their names, and so I'll call them Mary and David. They were English, from somewhere in the south, I recall, and were returning home, via Hong Kong, from a six-week trip to Australia. I didn't mind listening as they told me of their adventures. It helped the time go by and it also helped settle my mind. Worries and concerns about my daughter faded to the back of my mind.

Eventually dinner was served, and it was only then, realizing for the first time how much they had been talking about themselves, that Mary asked me what I had been doing in Hong Kong.

I told them a little about Samantha and her job at the hotel, then Mary asked if I worked. So I found myself telling them what I did.

"Ooh," said David, grinning at his "mother," "you like that kind of stuff, don't you, Mary?" Then he added, "No offense, but I don't believe in any of it."

I laughed, used to this reaction, and said no offense was taken. At this point the stewardess came to clear dinner, and it was a good opportunity for me to withdraw from the conversation.

"Well," I said, "I think I'm going to read for a while, then try to get some sleep."

Mary agreed that sleep was a good idea, and within minutes she was fast asleep.

David watched the movie and I read for a while, then, wrapping my blanket over me and reclining my seat back as far as it would go, I settled down, hoping that I would be able to sleep for at least a few hours.

The lights of the plane were dim, and snores and grunts could be heard over the drone of the plane's engines as people slept. I changed my position, trying to find a more comfortable spot in the narrow, cramped seat, pushed my pillow around a little, and closed my eyes. Sleep, sleep, I prayed, let me sleep.

Tap, tap, tap, on my shoulder. I ignored it. A few minutes went by.

Prod, prod, prod, harder now. I refused to acknowledge the finger, pushing, insistent, on my shoulder.

Several more minutes passed. I could feel myself beginning to drift. Oh, if I could only sleep.

Tap, tap, tap. Not again. I thought, "Go away."

Prod, prod, prod. That finger again.

"Leave me alone," I muttered. "I'm trying to sleep, can't you see? Go away, whoever you are, I'm sleeping."

"I'm his brother, David's brother. I know you can hear me. Just tell him I'm here."

"Look," I said, more angrily now, "can't you see I'm trying to sleep? I don't care who you are. I'm tired, so go away."

Five minutes. Ten minutes. At least fifteen minutes passed. I was just beginning to fall ... mmm, what bliss ... then, his voice again.

"I want to talk to my brother. I want to talk to David. My name is Michael. I'm his twin brother, and I died of cancer over twenty years ago."

Too tired to be angry now, and desperately needing sleep, once again I told this night intruder to go away. "Only if you promise to talk to me in the morning," he said firmly. "Otherwise I'll keep pestering you all night."

Blackmail, this is blackmail, I thought foggily, and you the reader might be wondering, as was I, where Grey Eagle was right now. But some things I have to learn to deal with. And besides, my guide knew that Michael and David needed this chance.

Now, more asleep than awake, I agreed, saying only that if the opportunity arose I would take it. With that I slipped mercifully into sleep.

Some four hours later, I woke. The early-morning sun was streaming in through the window, and for a moment I forgot where I was. Then the hum of the engines penetrated my muddled brain, and I pushed myself out of sleep and up into my seat. My two companions were already awake, and I heard the clatter of trays as the stewards served breakfast.

Our tables down, we chatted as we waited. When our food was served we all three attacked it as if it were some gourmet dish, instead of the poor-quality food so often served on airlines.

We were approaching the end of our meal before Michael made his presence known to me once more. Very shortly after that, Mary, reaching over her "son," said, "I hope you don't mind my asking, Rosemary, but I'm ever so interested in what you do. I know he makes fun of it," she went on, indicating David with a flick of her thumb, "but don't mind him. He doesn't know any better."

I smiled, waiting, knowing now that the time had come, then David said, "Well, what's there to believe? It's all guesswork really, isn't it?" He looked at me and grinned. "Go on, tell us—if it's real, tell us what you can see around us."

Many people over the years had said these same words to me: prove it, prove it. Usually, my response is to smile, shrug, and explain that I am not a puppet or some weird kind of entertainment. I say this without irritation, as I understand that many people see me as a curiosity. As for some, those with no understanding or willingness to understand, what am I to them . . . the organ grinder or the monkey? And their cry is simply, "Let's see the monkey dance." And so usually I ignore the "prove its."

But this time it was different. This time I had been waiting, knowing that there would be such a moment. Even so, I asked David, "Are you sure, are you really sure, you want me to 'show you'?"

He laughed at me kindly and winked, showing that to him this was just good fun, and nodded his assurance. There were, of course, other people on the plane, and I was aware that some were listening to our conversation. As I spoke it seemed that the chatter around us lessened, the more curious listening rather intently. But I could not worry about the reactions of others. My job now was to help Michael, although in my heart I hoped that what was happening might in some way help someone else.

With these thoughts I turned my attention fully now to the work at hand, and to David.

"I'm ready when you are," he chuckled. "Let's begin."

"There is a young man standing just behind you," I said, "and a little to your left. He tells me that he is your twin brother, Michael, and that he died of cancer several years ago, when you were both young."

At first, David maintained his grin, turning to his "mother," believing that we were playing a joke on him, that his "mother" had given me this information. He saw the shock on her face, then, quite suddenly, the grin disappeared, his face paled perceptively, and he began to choke out the words, "How do you know?"

171

Without waiting for him to finish, I continued, as Michael was now talking to me in a rush and I wanted to catch as much as I could of what he said.

"Michael tells me that the ring you are wearing," I said, pointing to his ringed finger, "is his. Is that right?" I asked, knowing, of course, that it must be.

Now dazed, David looked down at the ring. "No one knows that," he whispered. "No one. It belonged to Michael, and when he died it was the only thing he left behind. I've worn it ever since."

As he had been speaking, Mary had placed her arms around him. Now she pulled him to her, and they cried for a while together. Then David, curiosity overcoming his shock, turned to me again.

"What is he doing? What can he see? How can he hear . . . can he hear me?" Questions, more and more and more, came tumbling out of his mouth, and so for the next hour the two brothers talked nonstop. They talked about the house he had just bought, Michael describing it in detail, and also describing the things David planned to do in it. Michael described also how, shortly after he had passed, David's parents had died too, leaving him orphaned at sixteen, with no place to go, no home, no family. This, Michael explained, was when David met Mary, the mother of David's best friend. He told me how Mary had become a sort of surrogate mother, taking David in and caring for him. All these things and more Michael talked to David about, trying in his way, which is the way of many in the spirit world who know the need of survival evidence, to show his brother that they had not really been separated, certainly not in a spiritual sense, and that he had been a guiding force in David's life.

This last message was, for Michael and I hope for David too, the most important. It somehow seemed an appropriate time and place, several thousand miles up in the sky, for Michael to say to David, "Tell him I'm his angel."

And
Angels Came

I was in a small spiritualist church in the city of Lincoln in England. I was the speaker for the evening. It was sometime in late 1993, possibly early 1994, I don't quite remember, but I know that it was approximately eighteen months before I published my first book, which was first released in America.

It was a Sunday, and as in most spiritualist churches, the service this evening comprised the singing of hymns, a prayer to begin, and a little prayer of thanks to God. Then, as all visiting mediums do, I gave a philosophical talk, after which there was another hymn. I then began making communication with the spirit world and giving messages to the congregation.

The church was full, not one empty seat in the house. As I was about to begin communication with those in spirit, the church door flew open and down the aisle staggered a woman, well dressed, somewhere in her early fifties, attractive ... and decidedly somewhat the worse for liquor.

Her entrance was, to say the least, dramatic. Flinging her arms outward in a theatrical pose, her voice educated, striving to sound sober, she announced to one and all, "So sorry I'm late ... I've just 'flown in' from America." Slowly she stumbled down the aisle a little farther, looking for somewhere to sit. In a loud and some-what exaggerated voice, she announced again that she had just "flown in" from America.

My audience, initially stunned into silence by the proceedings, now tried to find her a place, but there was not a seat to be had. They didn't know whether to throw our obviously drunken visitor out or make her welcome, and consternation was written plainly on their faces. It was only when I suggested to the organist that he vacate his seat in the congregation and sit instead at his organ that the dilemma was resolved. I had taken charge, had taken responsibility for our visitor and allowed her in.

She made as much fuss and performance as it was possible to make, and when finally seated displayed a somewhat smug ex-pression on her face. She had been noticed.

As we all settled down and I once again began my communi-cation with the spirit world, I could not help noticing looks of disapproval of our latecomer on many of the faces of my congre-gation. These looks grew rapidly to real disdain as the evening progressed, for every time I gave a message my drunken friend would loudly make a comment.

"I'm coming to the lady over there"—I pointed to where I needed to be—"the lady wearing the pink sweater."

"I've got a pink bra on," the woman said loudly. "Will that do?"

Among shushings and tut-tuttings from all, I continued. Then another message. "I want to speak to the young man on the fourth row, on my right. Yes you," I said as he raised his hand. "I have a man in the spirit world who tells me he is your father. He died unexpectedly of a heart attack." This was accurate, and I continued the communication, giving many details, then: "Your father is talking to me about your car." I hesitated, wondering how, in a delicate way, I could say what I had been told to say. "Your father tells me that the car is a complete mess," I eventually said. But as

I was about to continue, our noisy visitor spoke up yet again. "You mean it's a bloody wreck," she called out loudly. And I couldn't help but smile, because those were the precise words which had been given to me by my spirit communicator.

But the congregation were now showing their irritation, and many were hissing loudly at her to be quiet or leave. In a valiant effort, on my behalf, to restore peace and harmony in their church, they had inadvertently created disharmony, and had become a greater distraction to my work.

For a few moments I watched, assessing the situation. Then, as respectfully as I could, I asked for quiet. Making it clear that I could, and would, handle this situation in my way, I spoke gently to our guest. "Could I ask," I said, smiling at her, "that you try to stay as quiet and still as possible? For you see, it is upsetting to everyone when you interrupt."

Her eyes grew wide with innocence, as if she had not known that this was the case, then, placing a finger to her lips, she nodded her agreement.

From then on I continued with no further hindrance, and eventually the last prayer was said and the service came to a close.

As is usual in the spiritualist churches I have visited, tea and biscuits were then served and a small social gathering was formed. At this point I retreated to the platform, to sit for a few minutes and rest. But my rest was short-lived, for only moments later I was joined by the woman "from America," who, smelling heavily of drink, sat herself beside me and without ado placed her head on my shoulder. My hand went out to her instinctively, and as I stroked her hair I talked softly to her, telling her I was glad that she had come and asking how we could help her.

After a while she straightened herself up, and once again, in a voice less strident but still slurring her words, she told me how she had just flown in from America. Then, in a voice much softer now, she spoke my name, and now there was something about her which was much different. I looked at her and could see that she was no longer drunk, but totally sober, and her gaze as she looked into my eyes was at the same time intense and gentle.

"Rosemary," she said softly now, but almost urgently, "Rosemary . . . they sent me to look at you . . . they sent me from America to look at you."

There was no trace of the woman who had pushed her way drunkenly through the door earlier, of the woman who had constantly interrupted the service. As I gazed back into her eyes I had the startling revelation that she was not drunk at all, just playing a part, a role, and I knew that she had indeed "been sent."

Our intimacy lasted only briefly, for I then felt a hand on my arm, and one of the congregation asked if I would like a cup of tea. I turned to thank her and said yes I would, and as I did so I heard again the sharp strident tones and slurred words of a drunk, and watched as my late visitor staggered drunkenly from the church, not even a backward glance in my direction. As suddenly as she had come, she was gone.

I sat for a few moments longer, remembering her words and the way she had looked at me, then I stood and gave my attention to those others who had come to hear me speak.

During the rest of the evening I made several inquiries of the regulars of the church. No one had seen our visitor before, no one knew her name or where she had come from, and since that time, to my knowledge, she has never visited that church again, and I have never seen or heard from her since.

I have thought of this incident often, and particularly when I am asked questions about angels.

She came to me with a message, less than two years before my first book was published in America. She came to tell me they were watching me, watching my progress, watching over me. She came disguised as a drunk, a nobody, seemingly fallen by the wayside.

She was a traveler, a messenger, a messenger from God ... and of this I am sure ... she was an angel.

I believe that angels come to us in many forms, in many guises, that they are of this earth as surely as they are of heaven. I believe that the stranger who smiles a greeting as you walk down the street could be an angel. I believe that the tramp who you might see scavenging through trash cans could be an angel, the woman you see begging, the snot-nosed child ... and I believe our streets hold many angels. And how aware are we that they exist and are among us? If we look at a recent survey taken in the United States, and if we look at the sales of books about angels, it would seem that we all of us, or at least 85 percent of us at any rate, believe in and accept that angels are real. But how real?

Many times when describing the moment of death, those in the spirit world mention the presence of angels. So often, and especially with children, I will hear it said, "... and angels came, and they carried me gently to a safe place." And as you read this, many of you will nod, smile knowingly, accepting that this is so. "And angels came, and they carried me to a safe place."

And angels came ... and will continue to come, for as long as there is God, for as long as there is love, then there will be light ... and angels.

As I hear those in the spirit world talk of angels I cannot doubt the existence of such beings, and I know that they live within the light which is God energy. I know too that they are God's messengers, but it was not until three years ago in 1994 that I felt comfortable discussing my beliefs and feelings on the subject of angels. So deep is my respect and awe of such beings, so spiritually moved am I when speaking of them, that even as I write I am reminded of how in the ancient scriptures the telling of a story began: "And it came to pass ..."

And so ... it came to pass that a woman whom we shall call

Anna, a client, called me from America, from somewhere in Connecticut, for a consultation, her third. I was in England, and we began the consultation in the usual way. First I asked Anna who in the spirit world she would like to connect with, mother, father, brother, and so on. Then I asked what her questions to them would be if we were successful in making contact.

At first her questions were the usual ones. After asking for contact with her mother she requested guidance with her children, her girls, and perhaps advice on her career and her husband's health. Then, somewhat tentatively, she asked if it would be possible to know if she had her own special angel, and if so, what his or her name was, and how she could become more sensitive to this being.

I had never been asked this question before, and thinking it might not be an easy issue for me to deal with effectively, and also aware that Anna's mother was waiting to communicate, I placed this question last, thinking it probable that we would not have enough time to answer it.

How wrong I was. Quickly and easily Anna's mother dealt with all of the issues she knew her daughter needed help with. Then she gave Anna messages from herself and others in the spirit world, messages of love and comfort and reassurance of the existence of life after death. And the session was over. Anna's mother said her goodbyes and I was about to finish. At this point I was so engrossed with Anna's family that I had completely forgotten about the last question.

"But wait," said Anna, as I too was about to say goodbye. "What about my angel question? Could we please make time, Rosemary? It is so important to me and I have been thinking about it so often lately."

"Well, I'll try," I replied, "but I'm not too sure I'll be successful. However . . . wait, I can see a lady." And I began to describe her: "Short, slim, with gray-white hair, very ordinary-looking, and the most beautiful smile."

I began to ask her what connection she had with Anna, a grand-mother perhaps, or an aunt. "But wait," she said, and her voice was light, like music . . . "and look at me." And with that she began to turn around.

At first I couldn't believe what I was seeing, it was so unex-pected. I closed my eyes, then quickly opened them again, and sure enough the vision was the same: I saw wings . . . angel's wings. Now she turned to face me, chuckling at my surprise, and nodding her head, her eyes twinkling, she said, "My name is Mary, and yes . . . I am her Angel. Tell her this, and tell her also that she has known of my existence for some time now, ever since she became curious to know if I was here. And in her knowing, and with patience and with time, she will come to know me better."

I listened in awe, repeating to Anna all the angel said. Then came the last message, said with feeling, and with deep affection, words I will never forget. And as the Angel uttered these words I saw the light around her as it grew, and as it grew brighter it seemed to envelop me as I repeated her words to Anna . . . and so it came to pass that the angel spoke, her voice soft, her smile gentle, her message to Anna clear: "Joy, oh greatest of joys, that you should finally ask for me."

But again I ask, "How real? How real and involved in our lives do we really believe angels to be? When we are faced with them, in books, or in pictures, or when we hear others speak of them, we know and understand the reality. Otherwise, for most of us, myself included, out of sight means out of mind. I am more fortunate than most in that during the course of my work I am constantly reminded. It is easier for me . . . I see. And I wonder, how can I help others to see?

And how are we supposed to recognize them if we don't know what to look for? All we know is that they are God's messengers, that they come from light, and that they are good, and pure of heart.

Perhaps this is the secret. That they are pure of heart. Maybe this is the way forward for all of us who are yet mortal. Suppose all that angels need from us is that we learn to look at ourselves and each other in a new way. That we learn to look for the purity and goodness of the soul. Surely, if we strive to practice this in our everyday lives, if we can somehow learn to live our lives giving unconditional love to our fellow men and women, then maybe, just maybe, our angels, when we meet them, might give us some small sign of their presence . . . and then joy, oh greatest of joys, we who for so long have lived our lives blinded will finally see them.

I believe that the stranger who smiles a greeting as you walk down the street "could" be an angel.

I believe that the tramp who you might see scavenging through trash cans "could" be an angel.

The woman you see begging.

The snot-nosed child.

Perhaps you are sitting next to an angel now.

Maybe last night or this morning you brushed past an angel as you hurried about your day.

This could be the time to take a moment and wonder. If you knew that today you might meet an angel, what would you say? What kind of attitude would you want to have? And how would you like your angel to see you?

I believe that angels are all around us.

I believe they wait at every corner.

I believe that angels are of earth as they are of heaven.

I believe they wait for us to see them.

And angels came . . . for as long as there is love, then there will be light . . . and angels.

Michael

I was in Los Angeles with my publicist Tina, on tour, promoting *The Eagle and the Rose*. There had been so many cities, so much travel, racing from plane to plane, taxi to hotel, hotel to taxi. All the places were beginning to merge into one in my head.

My only thought was "Whatever needs to be done to promote the book, I'll do." My determination and resolve gave me the strength to do just that. But that was not the only thing that kept me going, for along this journey I met many people, many who had great need of my message and the truth that I carry. And it was my experiences with these people that truly inspired me to go on when the need for sleep and rest overwhelmed me.

I had to be at a TV studio at a place called Eagle Rock. An apt name, don't you think? As we walked out of the hotel our chauffeur for the day came to meet us and ushered us to the car. He was very tall, easily six feet six, and I felt dwarfed by him.

On the drive to the studio, which took over an hour, Tina, my publicist, Ann, our tour guide, and I sat discussing the various events of the day. The schedule was fairly easy. A TV show, then back to the hotel for a print interview, lunch, then a drive along the coast to a bookstore where I was to lecture and sign books that evening.

As we discussed the format of the TV show, Tina recounted some of our experiences at other bookstores, how she had watched with amazement when she heard me give messages from the spirit world and witnessed the audience reactions.

Our chauffeur had said nothing on our journey, but I knew he was listening intently to our conversation. So on our arrival at the studio I invited him to come in and watch. He was a little flustered by the offer, but nevertheless came with us into the television studio.

The show lasted thirty minutes, and then we immediately piled back into the car and made our way to the hotel. The chauffeur had watched the show but made no comment. His only response was a quizzical look in my direction as we headed back to town.

After lunch, Tina and I decided that a nice easy drive along the coast road on our way to the book signing was a great idea, and so we again headed out to the waiting car. The chauffeur held the car door open and helped me inside. Just as Tina was about to climb into the car she remembered some paperwork she needed to fax to the office. A little awkward and embarrassed, she asked if I would mind waiting. "Not at all," I smiled, "take your time, I'll talk to the chauffeur while I wait."

At that, the chauffeur turned his head a little to look at me, and I smiled at him my reassurance. I knew he had something he needed to say to me.

"I lost my son," he began falteringly, as Tina scurried off. "He died in my arms."

"Michael," I said gently. "I'm hearing the name Michael."

"That's me," he replied, "and my son's name is Michael too."

And with that he began to tell me his story. His son, Michael Junior, had been sick for some time. He had had a great deal of treatment, had been hospitalized. On his final journey to the hospital he had died in his father's arms. In his late teens, early twenties, young Michael was just beginning, he had his whole life ahead of him, and it was snatched away. This was how his father saw it.

"As I held him in my arms, he said, 'Dad, I love you,'" Michael told me, and he continued, "I tightened my arms around him and, choked with emotion, I said, 'Son, I love you too.' With that I looked at his face. His eyes were closed, a single tear ran down his cheek, and I knew that he was dead. It was the only time in my life," said Michael ruefully, "that I have ridden in the back of a limousine instead of driving one."

As I had been listening to Michael, Tina had come back to the car, and had been listening also. She sat in the back with me, and I could see she was having a hard time keeping herself from crying, for our chauffeur's sadness and pain were very apparent.

Yet one more tragic story. And life is full of them, but that does not in any way lessen the pain of the individual, and as we sat listening to Michael's story it was easy for me to reach out a comforting hand, and to absorb some of the pain that this father was feeling for the loss of his son.

Eventually we journeyed on, our chauffeur now more than the driver of the car, for as we had shared those painful moments, he and I, a bonding had occurred, and now we were friends.

We drove down the coast road, slowly, so that I could get a real sense of where I was. It was beautiful, and just what I needed to energize me and prepare me for the evening's work.

Finally we arrived at our destination. This bookstore was unusual in that it had a room large enough to seat three hundred people, and it was packed.

I had given Michael the option of either going off by himself or coming in to hear the lecture. I felt that the latter might help him, but I was very careful not to push the idea, as I firmly believe that each of us has to come to our spiritual path in our own time.

Michael decided to take a break, so, agreeing that he would pick us up in two hours, we went our separate ways, mine, of course, into the bookstore.

As I was ushered by the store manager into the room, it was pleasing for me to hear the hubbub of excited voices, men and women, perhaps not knowing what to expect from the evening, but all eager to hear, to learn, and all hopeful. It was, I felt, a good atmosphere, warm and friendly, and positive energy was bouncing off the walls.

I went to my chair at the front of the room and watched as people found their seats. All were taken, and many had to stand, and in fact people were spilling out of the doorway and into the bookstore. To see such a turnout was very gratifying for me, and instinctively I knew it was going to be a special night.

As always at such events, I spoke a little about myself and my work, then, liking audience participation, announced a question-and-answer time. This part of the evening is always the best for me, as I like the interaction with my audience, and messages from the spirit world are often given.

This night was no exception. All there were eager to join in, and many from the spirit world came to join us and to give us their messages.

It was perhaps halfway through the evening when one young man there asked, "Rosemary, tell us about spiritual healing. Tell us, please, how you work."

Always willing to talk about my healing work, and my organization, the RAAH, I began first by telling one or two stories of the patients I have around the world. Then, knowing I could do better, I decided to "show" my audience, explain not by words but by actions.

Earlier in the evening I had noticed, as I had watched people entering the room, a lady, in her late seventies or early eighties, obviously struggling to find her way, being helped to a seat on the front row. Now, microphone in hand, I went up to her and, taking her hand, knowing she was here for this, I explained to my audience that I would demonstrate the gift of healing.

Now before I go further with this story, I must stop a moment to remind you that healing, first and foremost, is given to the spirit self, the light or energy field that surrounds the soul. Rarely does the onlooker see more than one person laying hands upon another. It is more a sense, a feeling of peace and light, which tells us that something is happening.

So here I was, about to display my gift, understanding that if my audience expected some Christlike miracle they would likely be disappointed.

As I held my new patient's hand and talked to this gathering, it occurred to me that maybe they could help me, and learn a little too. This was fun, this was real audience participation. Asking everyone there to hold hands, I described how they too could give their energy, their healing energy, to my patient.

Slowly I talked them through the simple first steps a healer learns, explaining how each person can develop, create, and use constructively that healing energy we are all born with. And as I talked, and as I gave, they gave to themselves, they gave to those around them, they gave to me, and they gave to my patient.

This healing session lasted perhaps five minutes, but those five minutes were intense in the gentlest way, and powerful. As I watched, I saw the light, I saw the love, it filled the room, and to my delight as I looked around, I saw my chauffeur, Michael—he had obviously been there all evening. And not one person there was separate, and in unity we all gave.

Knowing that there was more work to do, more questions to be asked, more messages to be given, and knowing that my patient had been given all she needed, I closed the healing session down. As I was about to move back to my place on stage and was thanking my patient for her cooperation, the old lady asked, "Can I please say something?"

A little surprised, I handed her the microphone. The audience, hushed, wanting to hear her reaction to her healing, were stunned and moved to tears, as I was, by her words.

"I am a registered blind person," she began, "and when I walked into this room I could see only shadows, and everything was gray. Now I can see the pictures on the wall, I can see the colors. I can see"—she pointed to me—"that your blouse is green, and I can see the buckle on your belt. I never expected anything for myself when I came here," she continued, "I only came to listen, but I would like to thank you all, and I would like to thank God, for the miracle you have given me tonight."

Rarely, as I said earlier, does a healer or an onlooker see or be present to witness a miracle. But here, for all of us to share, was that Christ-like miracle that all healers hope and pray for, and every one of us in the room was touched by it.

As the evening progressed there were more questions and more messages from the spirit world, messages of hope and inspiration. The final message, though, was for me the most special, as a child, a young girl who had died in very tragic circumstances, came through from the spirit world to talk with her mother. As I spoke of the child to her mother, and as I relayed messages from the girl to her family, I was able to give the mother of this girl clear evidence that her daughter had survived death. And in doing that I was able to bring comfort to all those people in the audience that their loved ones in spirit were safe, to bring hope to those in the audience who had lost their children also.

I looked to where Michael stood, and smiled at him, knowing that he finally understood that his boy had survived death and was safe.

After the event was over, we were tired and hungry. Michael drove Tina and me to one of the nicer hotel restaurants for a late dinner, and as I knew that he hadn't eaten either, I insisted that he join us. He was at once both flattered and a little embarrassed, but we soon put him at ease, and the evening, although late, was very enjoyable, for it was an opportunity that Michael had been waiting for.

It was an evening of questions and answers. Questions from a father needing to know and to understand his son's survival. Answers, not always conclusive, from me and from Grey Eagle, trying in some small way to fill his need. And it was an evening of souls on this earth, of different cultures, different backgrounds, coming together in spiritual communion, to share God's wonder.

I have told this story, not satisfied that I have conveyed to you the specialness, the moving moment, of that one evening, of what it meant to me. Often in my life I meet the unexpected and have learned that what might seem unplanned is, in fact, all part of God's great plan. So it was no surprise to me that Michael came into my life, for this oh so brief moment of time, in the way that he did. But there is something about this story, his story, that reaches a place deep down in my heart, and I will always be grateful for the experience of meeting him.

I have not seen or heard from him since that day, but I think of him sometimes, I remember his face, and I feel again one small moment of joy.

Angel in
the Cellar

A mutual friend introduced us, and I liked them from the start. Sandra was Australian and Alan, her husband, was Scottish. This was a second marriage for both of them, and for the most part they had lived in Australia, but Alan became homesick and so here they were, both in their early forties, no job, no work. Having spent two years in England trying to build some kind of life, and having failed, they were planning to return to Sandra's home.

It worked out perfectly. I needed someone to take care of my house for the next several months, winter months, and Sandra and Alan needed a place to live.

As I didn't know them, I decided that it would be a good idea if they moved in with me for two or three weeks before I left on my trip to the Far East. Grateful for the suggestion, Sandra and Alan agreed. This turned out to be a great idea. We got along splendidly, had roughly the same views on housekeeping, and, most important, they loved my dog, Karma, whom I was also leaving in their care.

To my surprise, although I should not have been surprised at all, and to my delight, they were more than interested in my work. There were many late nights as we sat drinking coffee and chatting into the early hours about the meaning of life, of God, and of all those other meaningful things. And it was on one of these nights that Alan tentatively suggested that he and Sandra would love to be invited to sit in on one of my Friday-night healing classes.

Visitors are rare on class nights, although I encourage anyone to visit our healing centers. However, I knew that Sandra and Alan's interest was real, not just mild curiosity, and so even though I told them I would think about it and let them know, I had already made my decision.

The following Friday came around, and I knew that this would be the night. I knew also, as I sat with Sandra and Alan at dinner, prior to the meeting, that something special was going to happen for them, but I didn't know what.

At 7:30 p.m. my class filed in, and I introduced our visitors. Always delighted to share, my students were pleased to welcome them, and for the first twenty minutes or so each student told the story of how he or she had become involved with our organization.

Gradually, as I listened to my students talking, I became aware of a strong presence, other than Grey Eagle, in the room. I felt that familiar feeling which precedes trance, and wondered only mildly that I would be going into a trance state in front of strangers, for Sandra and Alan were certainly strangers to the environment we were in now.

Trusting Grey Eagle, trusting that this was the right action, slowly I allowed myself to sink into trance. My students, ever watchful, had become quiet now, had drawn close to me, anticipating spirit communication, safeguarding me with their prayers, at the same time confident of my safety, trusting the process.

She moved into me with a grace and gentleness I acknowledged but hardly felt, and then I became the watcher as she eased herself more boldly into the body I had now vacated. I watched as my fingers moved, small movements, but not my movements. Grunting, coughing noises came from my mouth, as if I were clearing my throat. But they were not my sounds.

189

My students knew to wait, and strangely, Sandra and Alan, probably affected by their calm, knew to wait also, even though (they told me later) they felt their hearts pounding a little louder, and their throats become suddenly dry.

Again the coughing sound, some small movement of her/my head, and then, without looking up: "I am the little old lady with no teeth"...this said softly but firmly, and my students, for all there had experienced her before, smiled their delight and amusement. Always when she came to visit us she would introduce herself this way. Often she would make us smile with her complaint that "she," meaning me, had "too many teeth" for her liking.

Our "visitor" was a character. A great teacher, remarkable in her wisdom, always tough on her/my students, she came to talk to us only rarely. Her perspicacity, her brilliance as a teacher, and her inspiration were a true gift to us. Her sharpness, her aptitude for getting precisely to the point, fast, kept us all, including me, alert and on our toes.

Now she was talking to us again, or more accurately, she was talking to our visitors. "Sandra, Alan, welcome. We have been waiting for you...we have been waiting, Alan, for you."

Alan looked up, startled by being singled out, nervous about his responses, not wanting to put a foot wrong. He knew, without knowing how he knew, that a great revelation was coming to him, about what he didn't know, and he was both nervous and eager at the same time.

"Alan...Alan," our "teacher" called again, "do not be afraid. We know your story and must tell it to you now, so you will know we know you.

"We will take you back some many years, to the time, Alan, when you were a child, a small child, just three or four years old. Your parents argued often, then your father left, leaving you in the care of your mother. It was a big house you lived in, Alan, wasn't it, a big rambling old house, and the two of you lived there alone."

Alan nodded, more nervous now, and now with even more anticipation.

"Alan ... Alan ..." again our teacher called. "Do not be afraid ... we know your story ... and must tell it to you now, so you will know we know you.

"Your father gone, your mother drinking, and you a child, and so alone ... and then the cellar ... then the cellar ... then the cellar ..."

Still the watcher, now I see that Alan is crying, softly, silently, tears rolling down his cheeks.

"Alan ... Alan ... do not be afraid," now gently I hear our "teacher" say. "We know your story ... and must tell it to you now, so you will know we know you."

And I the watcher, I the listener, watched and listened as Alan lowered his head in silent obeisance.

Alan's wife, her eyes wide with amazement, never having heard more than the bare bones of her husband's childhood, also seemed to understand that something special was coming for Alan, but also that this meant he would have to face his memories, which were painful to him. She carefully, and with great tenderness, placed her hand over his, showing her love and support without the need for words.

"Alan ... Alan," the voice of our spirit teacher called out yet again, and by now all there in the room knew she would speak those same words again. "We know your story ... and we must tell it to you now, so you will know we know you."

And I the watcher watched, and I the listener listened, and then before me, as in a vision, even as part of that vision, for it felt as if I were there, I was in "the cellar."

From a distance, vaguely I could hear the little old lady with no teeth, as if now narrating, as the story unfolded before my eyes. I knew my students, Alan and Sandra, could not see or be involved as I was, but I knew also that they were being told all, even as it was being projected before me.

191

It was dark, so dark that it was several seconds before I could adjust my eyes to the gloom. And it had the dank musty odor of rotting wood. Also it was cold, so cold, and I shivered, not liking the place, wondering why I was there.

A small movement caught my eye, and I looked toward a window, tiny and covered with dust, so much so that what light might have filtered through was blocked. Under the window I was just able to make out a wide concrete sill. On it was what looked like a small sack or bundle of ... clothes? I couldn't see clearly what it was, and struggled to see more clearly. And as I watched, and as I listened, I saw the bundle move, I heard the bundle ... whimper? Too big to be a cat ... surely not a dog, not down here, not down here, trapped in this terrible place.

Now, whispered words filtered through my mind, I heard our teacher yet again ... "must tell it to you now, so you will know we know you."

My attention moved back to the bundle on the windowsill, and then I knew, with awful certainty, just what it was.

Another scene connected in my head: I saw his mother, Alan's mother, pushing her child, her little child, down the cellar steps, saw the child, tearstains on his cheeks, and saw the fear in his eyes as the trapdoor lowered, slammed shut, blocking out the light and any form of life and warmth and comfort that he knew.

Instinctively I knew that this had been the pattern of his childhood, that this was not his mother's way to punish him, merely a place to put him, to keep him "safe" when she decided to take herself off. Sometimes she would leave him there for just a day, but more often she would be gone for three days or more, perfectly confident that he could come to no harm. I also knew she did this often, not just once in every year or two, but on a fairly regular monthly, sometimes weekly, basis.

Words, words, floating down around me ... "Story ... story ... tell it to you ... so you will know we know you."

The bundle moved again, stretched a little, whimpered, curled up, and went back to sleep...but only for a moment.

Her voice again, now sharp and clear, but soft and gentle too, bringing me back, not yet from the cellar, for hard as it is to explain, I was in the cellar and at the same time back with my students, back in class. The old lady, still using my body, my voice box, continued on, describing the state of terror the child was in as he lived those terrible dark days, describing his bewilderment and fear that perhaps one day his mother would forget him, that like his father, she wouldn't come back. Then, to Alan, who sat remembering, who sat in pain and anguish, she said, so softly now, "Alan, remember your friend...remember your friend?"

And I the watcher, and I the listener, saw and heard. His head came up, and for just one moment I saw confusion in his eyes, and then he gasped and remembered all, and recognition and realization came to him, and for the boy that he had been, and for the man that he was now, there was no more fear, and only joy. And as he wept, and as Sandra wept, and as all there cried with him, we could only rejoice.

I hear yet another voice, this one a voice like music, sweet breath on the wind, and calling out his name, "Alan...Alan... remember me...remember me," and Alan, nodding, was suddenly healed.

My eyes moved back to the cellar, to the bundle I now knew to be Alan. The light had changed—was it perhaps a little brighter now? I wondered. Then that same sweet voice, like music, but coming from the cellar now, and calling Alan's name.

"Alan...Alan..." the sound floated through the air..."Alan ...Alan...wake up and play with me."

The child moved, and opening his eyes, he looked to where the voice had come from...and a bright light filled the room, spilling onto the walls and floor, spilling onto the child. "Come play with me, come play with me, and I will keep you safe."

Alan, the little boy, sat up straight on the wide concrete ledge, rubbed his eyes sleepily, stretched and yawned. "Alan ... Alan," came the voice again, and Alan, turning toward it, smiled, and jumped down off the ledge. "Will you play with me?" I heard him shyly ask. "Will you stay with me till Mum comes back?"

And I the watcher and I the listener watched and listened, and the light grew brighter still. And through the light I saw a figure, small and slim, a child almost but not a child ... and through the light I heard a voice, like music, sweet breath on the air ... "Alan ... Alan ... yes, Alan, I will play with you, and stay with you until your mother comes back, and after then, and all your life ... and all your life ... I'll keep you safe, I'll keep you safe."

Alan looked toward the child, yet not a child. He looked into the light.... "My name's Alan," he boldly ... shyly ... said. "What's yours?" And did I hear a sigh?

"Why, Alan, don't you know me? Oh yes, you surely do...."

I watched as two hands, four hands, reached, into, out of, the light, then I saw them join, and all was light.

"Alan ... Alan," and the voice ... sweet music, filled the air, and filled every fiber of my being, the sound of love, pure love.... "Why, Alan, I'm your angel."

Part V

LAWS OF THE UNIVERSE

THOSE OF YOU WHO READ MY FIRST BOOK WILL EXPECT THAT IN this and in all my future books you will hear the wisdom of my guide, Grey Eagle. There are many questions that I, and others, have put to him over the years, questions that range from the universal and cosmic to the specific and often seemingly mundane. Many of his answers will seem, on first reading, to be complex, others too simple, and others still, may seem not to be answers at all. But I have found, over time, that whatever his answer to a question may be, and however we may agree or disagree with what he says to us, his desire is to lead us to our own answers, our own conclusions. So it is with this thought that I will continue on.

Searching

I was in Italy in January 1996, on a book tour, which meant four days of intensive media interviews. The days were planned precisely, to get the best and most of my time, and consequently sightseeing and shopping were out of the question. Well, that was okay, although it saddened me that I was in such a beautiful city as Rome and was unable to experience it. However, I was, after all, there to work.

But there was one place I felt I simply must visit, especially as this was my first time in Italy. I didn't quite know how I could do it, but I knew I wouldn't leave without seeing the Sistine Chapel. My publicist was great, and when I told her how important it was to me, she managed to organize an early-morning visit. "As long as we are back in the hotel for the first interview," she said, and delighted, I agreed.

Those of you who have visited the Sistine Chapel will know that its beauty is indescribable. That beauty is everlasting, imperishable, immortal, a work of art made more splendid by its holiness. And as I stood in the middle of the room, with only a few people milling about, and as I gazed at the painting behind the altar, I felt a great need to be alone in there, alone with God, with

Christ, and with Grey Eagle. But that was not possible...or was it?

I looked about and noticed there were benches on either side of the chapel, most of them empty. Slowly, I moved to one of them and sat down. Then, closing my eyes for just a moment, I raised my level of conscious thought, to a place above and beyond that which is earthly, while still being of the earth and still seeing that of the earth which I needed to see.

My eyes were drawn again to the painting behind the altar, which filled almost the entire wall. I could now see nothing else. And I looked, and looked, and I realized that what I saw was so much pain, and so much suffering, of all mankind. *The Last Judgment*, by Michelangelo, and this was how he saw it.

I was moved, so moved by this, and was easily able to relate that suffering to the torment and anguish I see in the lives of so many, every day. And forgetting for the moment all the joys and all the wonders of our world, I whispered softly to my God, and to my Christ, and to my guide, Grey Eagle, "Why, why..." As tears trickled down my face, I asked, "Why must it be this way? Why must it always be this way?" And through my tears, and through my pain, the pain of that one moment, I heard a voice. It softly called to me, "But pain is your great teacher."

I sat for moments longer, knowing this, accepting this. A great sigh escaped my lips, and whispering my thanks, I left.

I began searching. The Bible, I thought, that must be where I begin. Then I was reminded of a story I'd heard.

A very religious woman went into a bookstore and asked the assistant for a Bible. "Certainly, madam," replied the young man, and reaching behind him, he took from the shelves several books. Laying them on the counter, he said, "We have the King James Version, or the New Revised Standard Version, or the Good News Version, or the New American Standard Version. Which would you like"? The woman, righteous and angry, leaned across the counter, "I don't want any of 'your' versions, I want the Bible as God gave it!"

So, which Bible should I choose? Well, a friend had bought me the New Revised Standard Version, so I began there. But what was I looking for? I wasn't really sure. Rules? Guidance? Rules... I must start with rules, so turning to Exodus, Chapter 20, I discovered again, for the first time since my teenage years, the Ten Commandments, given by God, through Moses.

Exodus 20:2–17

Then God spoke these words to Moses. "I am the Lord your God, who brought you out of the land of Egypt, out of the house of slavery."

1. You shall have no other gods before me.
2. You shall not make for yourself an idol....
3. You shall not make wrongful use of the name of the Lord your God....
4. Remember the Sabbath day and keep it holy....
5. Honor your father and mother....
6. You shall not murder (or kill).
7. You shall not commit adultery.
8. You shall not steal.
9. You shall not bear false witness against your neighbor.
10. You shall not covet your neighbor's house, you shall not covet your neighbor's wife, or male or female slave, or ox, or donkey, or anything that belongs to your neighbor.

I read on. In Chapter 21, God continues, giving Moses rules concerning slaves. Verse 2: "When you buy a male Hebrew slave, he shall serve six years...." Verse 7: "When a man sells his daughter as a slave..." Chapter 22, Verse 2: "If a thief is found breaking in, and is beaten to death, no blood-guilt is incurred." Verse 3: "But if it happens after sunrise, blood-guilt is incurred." Verse 16: "When a man seduces a virgin who is not engaged to be married, and lies with her, he shall give the bride price for her, and make her his wife."

I read on. Verse 29: "The first born of your sons you shall give to me...."

I read still a little further, and am somewhat confused, until I remembered how long ago it was that Moses went up Mount Sinai. I remember his people, simple, uncomplicated, uncluttered, and not confused by the discoveries of modern-day science.

So what am I saying? I ask myself, thinking out loud on the page. For if I write this chapter at all, I must be as honest with my reader as with myself. So what am I saying? Am I saying that the rules that Moses gave are outdated, of no use in our modern world? Do I think that the principles are good, but that the actual words do not apply? Maybe that's it...but I am not yet sure. Should I discard the Ten Commandments? Are they too outdated? Is my questioning of them audacious? Should I even be writing this at all? And how is it, I ask myself, that I never questioned this before? Is my respect of God, of my church, so strong that I accept in silent obeisance all things which have been given to me?

But then I am reminded...my church taught me to question, my teachers in school taught me to question. I am who I am because I am a curious and interested questioner.

I put down the Bible and reach for the next book. *When Prophets Spoke,* by the Rev. G. Maurice Elliott, published first in 1938, this edition in 1987. Hmmm, perhaps a more modern approach. I open to the Preface, which begins, "This book is a serious attempt to understand the so-called miraculous and theophanic elements in the Old Testament." In this book the author considers the possibility that Moses was a medium, for how else, he thinks, could Moses have communicated with God? He also mentions further in the book that Jesus too was a medium, was psychic. This is not a new thought for me, because I have wondered this myself.

Is this thought a blasphemous one? There are many who will think so, but it is not intended to be. I am merely thinking, questioning, out loud. Trying, like the Rev. G. Maurice Elliott, to understand.

I reach for the next book, one I was given many years ago, but have never read, not even one page. I have no idea what I will find, I am even somewhat puzzled at this moment about why I am searching.

The Dead Sea Scrolls Uncovered, by Robert Eisenman and Michael Wise. On the front cover the claim "The First Complete Translation and Interpretation of 50 Key Documents withheld for over 35 years." The book is published by Penguin.

I read, I read, and I really try to understand some of what is written here, but come to the conclusion that this book is written by scholars for scholars, which I am not. However, I do take something away with me. This is a clear reminder to me that I must, as a writer, keep my text simple so that I will be as little misunderstood as possible.

I move on, still searching. I reach now for *The Embodiment of Love, Sathya Sai Baba*, by Peggy Mason and Ron Laing.

My eyes skim the contents page, and I see what may be of help to me here: Book 2, Chapter 9, "The Living Principles of Sathya Sai Baba." The author, talking of Sai Baba, says: "The Principle which he applies to his contact with people is that of *absolute equality of all men under God*. Baba says, 'No society can find fulfillment until the spirit of man blossoms. The "Atma" in man has to be realized. The "Atma" is the sustenance, the source of every being, and every organization of beings. It is the one and only source. The "Atma" is God, no less. Therefore recognize in every being a brother, a child of God, and banish all limited thoughts and prejudices based on colour, status, class.' "

Continuing, I read: "Baba hates waste, and often reprimands his devotees for embellishing their shrine rooms so ostentatiously. 'Be simple and sincere' ... and to those devotees who claim they need a prayer hall, 'Why do you need a hall? Make your houses a shrine, impress others with your humility, speech, love, faith and truthfulness.'"

These, then, are the principles for living of Sai Baba. Voluntary, gradual, and individual means, rather than compulsory, instant, or collective. So writes Ron Laing.

These principles make sense to me. They speak of a day-to-day living of love and gentleness. The anti-dogma approach appeals to me much more than the "you shall not" approach which Moses used in the Ten Commandments.

What does the Pope think? I wonder. He seems such a gentle man. Is he anti-dogma, or rather the iron fist in the velvet glove? And what of the bishop, the head of the Church of England, the Archbishop of Canterbury, the Rev. George L. Carey? Is he anti-dogma?

My mind lingers awhile on these thoughts, before I realize that it really does not matter to me what others think, although perhaps it should, for these people are the dictators, aggressive or benign, of God's truths, God's laws. These are the men who influence the world. But remembering the violence and cruelty which invades our world, which these men seem not to affect, I move on. For now, it matters more what I think. I am struggling for some truth, some law, some direction.

And now I reach for *The World's Religions*, a Lion Handbook, first published in 1982. I scan the contents, and my eyes fall upon this passage.

HINDUISM

Hinduism has no founder, and no prophet. It has no particular ecclesiastical or institutional structure, nor set creed. The emphasis is on the way of living rather than a way of thought. Radhakrishnan, a former president of India, once remarked, "Hinduism is more a culture than a creed."

I think upon this for only a short time, but find my fingers turning the pages, and I search still more. Then...

BUDDHISM

And I begin to read.... In his third night of meditation under the bo-tree, Gautama discovered the Four Noble Truths. These are the core of Buddhist philosophy:

1. The first truth is the knowledge of suffering.

2. The second truth concerns the origin of suffering.

3. The third truth deals with the destruction of suffering.

4. The fourth truth indicates the way to the removal of this suffering.

This is by means of the Noble Eightfold Path, which formed Gautama's basic teaching on Buddhist life style.

Well, these are guidelines, rules to live by, for some at least, and, curious, I read on.

EIGHT SIGNPOSTS TO FREEDOM

1. Right knowledge or understanding—this of course means a recognition of the Four Noble Truths.

2. Right attitude or thought—indicates a mental attitude of goodwill, peaceableness, keeping far from oneself all sensual desire, hate, and malice.

3. Right speech—lying, useless chatter and gossip are outlawed; instead speech must be wise, truthful, and directed toward reconciliation.

4. Right action—embraces all moral behavior. *Murder, stealing,* and *adultery* are especially prohibited.

5. Right occupation—means that one's way of earning a living must not be harmful to others.

6. Right effort—Evil impulses must be prevented and good ones fostered, so that the individual can develop noble thoughts, words, and deeds.

7. Right mindfulness or awareness—means careful consideration, not giving in to the dictates of desire in thought, speech, action, and emotion.

8. Right composure—is achieved by intense concentration, which frees the holy man from all that holds him back in his quest.

All of this seems wise enough. The four truths remind me just a little of the Adam and Eve story, although I recognize that while God punishes Adam and Eve for disobeying, there is no mention of punishment in the four truths.

Could it be that my subconscious instantly and eagerly holds on to the idea that if man suffers it must be his own fault, that suffering is a punishment from God for some unknown sin committed by an unknown ancestor? And where did this idea come from? Childhood, perhaps, some Sunday-school story? I find it odd that I should even have this thought, as I definitely do not think that our sufferings on this earth are punishments from God. I realize once again, as I so often have, how deeply ingrained our childhood lessons are.

I am thinking out loud on paper, and I ask you to bear with me and my ramblings as I search on. Buddha's truths seem right and wise, leaving me feeling not dissatisfied, but certainly needing more ... and thinking. Also, in the way they are set out they remind me of Moses. Moses went up the mount. Buddha sat under the bo-tree. Both communicated with God.

So far I have heard God ... through Moses. I have heard God ... through Christ ... God ... through Sai Baba ... God ... through Buddha. Then ... God through the Pope. God through the bishop. Always there is an intermediary, some other person interpreting God's word.

Do I know Moses? Can I trust him?

Do I know Jesus? Can I trust him?

And what of Sai Baba, what of Buddha, the Pope, the bishop?

Do I know them? Can I trust them?

Of all these the only one I know is Christ. And how do I know him? It certainly wasn't through the Bible, or from other men's words. The Bible told me of him, men's words told me of him. But I came to "know" him through my own heart, searching not through the written word, but from my own experiences, from my own heart, my own mind, my own soul. And yes ... I trust Christ completely.

Now I have something. Now I have a truth. And now I have a direction too. If I truly want to discover the rules, the law or laws of the universe, I should perhaps seek them, as I did Christ, through my heart, my mind, my soul ... and I smile as I hear Grey Eagle say, as he has said so many times before, "There is not one question you can ask that you do not have the answer to, within your soul, your own soul."

So, should I discard other men's words, other men's truths? But there are many wise words, written by many wise and knowing men and women, of many different "religions," so rather than discarding all that I read, I will keep that which my heart acknowledges as good.

And speaking of other men's words, and of those I know and trust, and before I can draw any conclusions, or discover any truths about the laws of the universe, I must remember Grey Eagle, whom I know and trust, and I must remember his words, and his answers to some of the many questions which I and others have put to him over the years.

So we begin.

Questions

First I decide to ask Grey Eagle those questions that relate to religion.

Question: Grey Eagle, what is your concept of God?

Answer: I will repeat to you the many words which you may have heard before. And, knowing this, I know that I will leave you dissatisfied, for your concept is limited.

And so, I will tell you that God is all things to all men.

And God is the force which turns the universe.
And God is the force which breathes life into all things.
And God is the force which is truth.
And God is the force which is love.
And God is the force...
...and God is...
...and God...
God...

* * *

And as I hear his answer, I feel a stillness enter my being and fill my heart.

Question: Grey Eagle, there are many houses of worship on the earth plane ... churches, shrines, mosques, and temples, to name but a few. Is there an appropriate place to worship?

Answer: The universe hears your whisper ... the universe hears your cry ... and God, that all-knowing and all-seeing power, sees your heart.

Here, we have no use of shrines or temples. Here, we have no use of churches or mosques.

But for you who walk the earth plane ... if to sit in a temple helps to still your heart ... if to stay quiet in a mosque helps you to discover your soul ... if to walk through a quiet churchyard helps you to recognize the heart of your soul and to hear the heartbeat of the soul ... then we accept your need for such buildings as these.

But God will sit beneath a tree in a quiet meadow. And God will walk along a cool seashore. And God will enter a battlefield. And, yes, God will even visit a brothel, and sit by a drunken man, and stand close to the mother who whips her child.

There are many of you, on hearing my words, who will hold out your hands in horror at the thought of such things ... even while acknowledging that God is everywhere.

And even while acknowledging that God is everywhere, there are those of you who will hurry to your temples, your shrines, your places of worship, needing to be closer to him.

But most of all, I tell you, and truly from my heart, that there is not one being ... not one living thing ... that does not have God at its center, at the heart of it.

And there is no man, woman, or child who is exempt from this rule.

God's voice whispers to you through the trees. But, yet, if you live in a barren place where there are no trees, you may still, if you listen, hear his voice in the wind.

And God's breath blows to you on a cool breeze. But those of you who have no cool breeze and live in the heat of a city need have no fear, for, yet, still God's breath blows upon you and it will travel down the rays of the sun as easily as it will travel through the icebergs ... as easily as it will be carried by the snow-drifts ... as easily as it will ripple through the still waters of a quiet brook ... as strongly as it will call in the waves that crash down on a storm-laden shore.

And truly I will say to you, and from my heart, there is nothing that comes from the earth or that is given to the earth that God's hand does not touch.

And there is no one soul ... not one single soul ... that does not have God's heart within it somewhere.

So, build your temples and your shrines if this helps you to center yourselves and to discover your truth. For, whatever it is that you need ... and whatever it is that helps you to find your truth and to discover yourself ... then this, we feel, is a good thing.

• • •

I hear his answer, and am calmed. He does not say "we must" or "we must not," he does not deny us our right to choose. And I am reminded again of the wisdom of my guide.

Question: Grey Eagle, many of our world religions are governed by their own particular set of rules. Some of these religions teach that to break these rules is a sin, and God's punishment will be visited upon those who violate these rules. Grey Eagle, could we have your thoughts on this?

Answer: In all societies it is recognized that for the good of the many, certain rules are necessary. Within the universe, there are rules.

Within each and every society ... each and every sect ... it is understood that rules are necessary for the peace and harmony of the whole.

But any rule that has its roots in fear is a rule which is made by man and is not recognized by God ... is not recognized by the universe. The universe turns its back on no man ... on no soul.

No one soul, as we have said before, can be destroyed ... except if that one soul wills it. And we, who are of the Universe, do not mete out punishment. For who is to judge what is right and what is not right ... except the soul itself. It is the responsibility of each soul to accept that responsibility for itself. It is not for another to judge good or bad . . . right or wrong.

The universe does not punish; and I will say again, truly, and from my heart, God dwells within each of us . . . we who are of the spirit world . . . you who are of the earth plane. When God extends his hand, there are no limits.

And, I will say again . . . and firmly, so that you may hear me and understand . . . any rule which is based on fear is a rule that man makes and is not of God.

. . .

Again I hear Grey Eagle's words. I think now of Moses, of the Ten Commandments. I wonder again, briefly, which version of the Bible I have. I wonder, too, did Moses really give the commandments as they have been given in the Bible, or is this another man's interpretation? Of course, we know it is. So I must ask . . . how accurate is it? I will never know, and so I can only do one thing . . . I must listen to my heart.

Grey Eagle says, "The universe turns its back on no man . . . on no soul."

And this, knowing my God to be a loving God, this I believe.

Question: Grey Eagle, can someone be deeply religious but lacking in spirituality?

Answer: You will, again, use the word "religion," implying religious belief or religious behavior. And there is such a misuse of this word . . . and, yet, I understand your question. For what you are

asking is, 'Can someone have a deep-held belief in God...in
the Almighty...and the power of the Almighty and yet not
be a spiritual being?' My answer is that you may look through
many books, and you may read the word which you may understand to be God's word...you may listen to the words of your
teachers...you may hear these words and be inspired by these
words in your various beliefs...you may live from day to
day exactly in the way of the rules of your belief...and, yet,
still, if you have not recognized your soul and the heart of your
soul...and, still, if you have not heard the heartbeat of your soul
and moved, gently, with its rhythm...then how will your spirit
grow? For until you recognize and move with its rhythm, your
understanding of what is spirit and what is not spirit will be
lacking.

• • •

I hear his words, and smile, understanding how appropriate to my
exercise my guide's words are. And having put myself through this
exercise I understand more fully how wise and true his answer is.

I am reminded, too, that this question is double-edged. What
of those people who are good, caring, loving, living a good life in
a good way, but who do not recognize God, in any way? What
of their spirituality? Are they lacking?

From Grey Eagle's words I can deduce that recognition of one's
soul, one's spirit, comes not in the form of intellect, or of the
spoken word. Perhaps it is just sufficient to be. Perhaps it is
sufficient only to move to the rhythm of love.

I reflect again on Grey Eagle's answer.... "And, still, if you
have not heard the heartbeat of your soul and moved, gently, with
its rhythm...then how will your spirit grow?

For the first time since my search began, I feel I might be getting
somewhere. Of course, there will be some of you who will presume
that I am a little biased, that of course I will listen to Grey Eagle.

And you would be right to think that. But, like all of that which I have read so far, I will read Grey Eagle's words again and again, and I will question his answers, as he has taught me to, before I reach my conclusions, if any.

I feel now that I must address those questions which concern our beliefs and attitudes toward others. Listening to my heart, I know that no matter how controversial some issues are, I cannot complete my search for rules, for laws, if I don't test. After all, the only way we can really know whether a rule is a good one, a strong one, is to put it under pressure. And as Jesus himself taught . . . "If it is good it will flourish, and if it is bad it will wither away."

Before I continue, however, I must make it plain that the object of my exercise is to discover some truths, rules, laws, not for anyone else, but for me. I do not in any way mean to be arrogant, or disparaging of others' beliefs, or controversial just for the sake of controversy. I am simply looking for guidelines. And perhaps as I look, as I take you with me on this journey, you may find some guidelines for yourselves.

With that in mind, I move forward, prepared to ask Grey Eagle this next set of questions.

Question: Grey Eagle, why is there so much racial conflict on earth, especially in America? And do you see any positive solutions?

Answer: This question we will apply not just to one country, but to your world as a whole.

This question does, truly, not have too much to do with the color of the skin . . . although you will often, many of you, use this reason to see a difference in one man from another.

213

For the same attitude that a white man may turn his back on a black man is the same attitude that a white man may turn his back on a white man, and that a black man may turn his back on a black man.

It is the same attitude that those with much in the way of material possession will sometimes turn their back on those who have a very little in the way of material possession.

It is the same attitude that makes a Protestant turn his back on a Catholic.

The same attitude that causes racial conflict is the same attitude that causes religious conflict.

Race, creed, color, rich, poor, intellectual, unintellectual, striving, working, idle, able, unable ... all of these conflicts you have, which are rife in your world.

And there is one word which, in your language, you will understand, which will cover all of this and will tell you of a truth ...

... and that one word is *intolerance*.

And this will bring us back to the issue of God.

And this will bring us back to the issue that God is within each and every one.

And as you turn your back on another, whatever his position, whatever his race ... his creed ... his belief ... whatever his rank ... whatever his place is in your society ... if you turn your back on another, then, truly, God's eyes watch as you turn your back on him.

So caught up with your lives ... with your rushing and racing to be nowhere, thinking that it is somewhere ... so caught up with your rights and your wrongs ... and your man-made rules, which know little of God and the universe, and the workings of the universe, nor do they take into account the workings of the universe, and the workings of God, and that God Force which encompasses all of you ... so taken up with all of this are you that you become blind and panicked and fearful.

And so what better than to point the finger at someone else and to say if it were not for him ... or him ... or her ... or him ... or him ... then my world would be a better place.

And your reason, I will tell you and once again from my heart ...

... your reason for your confusion is fear.

Which of you may dare to take the mirror, which will show your true reflection ... that reflection which God sees ... and, even seeing, he loves you, yet, still.

And I will tell you ... take up the mirror that shows you your true reflection, and of the things that you will see that you will like ... encourage these things to grow within you; and of the things that you will see that you do not like ... then, remember, yours and yours alone is the responsibility.

And all is not lost. For you can change these things ... knowing that gentleness with your own self will help to do so.

• • •

I hear his words, and understand immediately how right he is. And I remember back to a time some fifteen years ago, to my

215

own fears. It was not long after Grey Eagle came into my life. Up to that point I had had many fears in my life, fear of failing, fear of speaking, fear of starving, fear of childbirth, fear of my father, of my mother, fear of the dark, and yes, I suppose, fear of being.

I had learned, over the years, to combat many of these fears, many of which we all have. I had feared the faces and voices which had followed me all my life, and now, having just begun to understand my life, there came another fear.

Each night I would go to bed, and as soon as my head touched the pillow, it came at me. A face, a force, an energy so fierce, so terrible. And laughter, evil laughter, as this "thing" would lunge at me again and again.

Terrified, calling out to my guide for help, I would switch on the light . . . but even that didn't stop "it," and I would lie trembling, night after night, week after week, afraid to close my eyes, wondering why Grey Eagle didn't protect me.

On the point of exhaustion, having had so little sleep for weeks, praying that this would be the night it would stop, I went to bed. I laid my head on the pillow, and closed my eyes, and there "it" was again, laughing, pushing its way toward me . . . and something happened, I just snapped, simply snapped. My tiredness had overtaken my fear.

"Go away," I shouted, and pushing my face up close, "I'm not scared of you, so just *go away* and leave me alone."

And an amazing thing happened. Before my eyes, the "thing," which had been such terrible energy, began to dissipate—not just disappear, but disintegrate, become no more. And I instantly realized that "it" had been feeding, feeding on my fear.

I sat up, shaking my head at my own inability to see, to know, to understand, that all it took, all it had ever needed, was my denial of "its" existence.

And it was then that I heard Grey Eagle's voice . . . and I remember his words to me then. With so much love and gentleness he spoke these words to me. "Child, know now, understand now, that the only *fear* you have to fear is *fear* itself."

Knowing this, accepting this, I can say to you, and with gentleness ... try each day to look in the mirror, past the lines and wrinkles, the spots and blemishes, past all those things which you wish were more perfect, and find yourself. Dare to do this, dare also to smile a gentle smile, and give love to yourself. Do this small thing each day, and you will find your soul, and you will find peace.

This next question is one I hesitated over, for so many people have such very strong opinions, and I do not seek to change those opinions. I am merely journeying, traveling upon a path I chose to walk.

And you may hear my guide's answer, and believe he says something against or for your own particular view, as with all his answers. And some may hear the question and refuse to read on, for fear of hearing a truth they may wish to deny.

But please remember, these are my questions, which I need to ask, questions not meant to cause hurt or harm, to give right or wrong, merely guidance for my own journey, and for enlightenment.

Question: Grey Eagle, there is a very heated debate going on in America right now between the pro-life and the pro-choice movements. If you were to address the activists of both movements, what would you say?

Answer: I would ask how it is that one human being ... one human soul ... should feel that he or she will have the answer to any specific question, not for his own self, but for all of mankind.

And I would ask you to ask what makes it so that one human soul should wish to force his will upon the will of another.

It is true that life itself is sacred. And it is true that life continues.

Those who claim that the aborting of a soul from a physical body destroys that life do not understand the strength of the soul ... of the spirit ... do not understand that the soul its very self cannot be destroyed unless, as I have already said, it chooses to be this way.

And who is to say that the soul its very self has not chosen to embark upon this journey, which you on the earth plane will consider to be so short a journey as to be nonexistent and a waste of ... in your language ... a waste of time?

It may be that a soul chooses to experience, for a brief span, what it will feel and what it will be within the womb of your living flesh ... for just a short span, and then to continue with its journey.

Who amongst you on the earth plane can say with such surety that this will cause damage to a soul, or end that soul's very being?

And how many of you will say, "Oh, yes, for I am God, for I know what God feels and what God thinks, and therefore I know what it is that God wills, not only for my own self but for all of mankind."

And, the earth shakes ... and the universe trembles ... yet, not with fear but, yet, with acknowledgment of the determination of some to press their will upon others.

Each must make his own choice.

And in understanding my answer fully, you first must understand that there are many reasons for a termination of life ... whether seemingly chosen by the individual ... the earth soul ... or whether chosen in another way.

And those of you who truly will hear God's voice will hear this voice clearly say, "Your will is a free will ... your spirit is a free spirit. I do not own it ... nor you ... nor do I own your thought ... nor do I own your heart ... nor do I own your soul, your spirit ... nor any part of you."

And God will call this out to you, and he will say again, "I do not own one part of you, nor would I have it this way. For each soul is its own master, and each soul dictates its own life its own way, and each soul will choose."

And if this soul chooses to give itself to God, then it is for that soul and that soul alone to make this choice ... and that choice is between the soul and God alone and for no other ear or eye to hear or see.

And there is no judgment.

And God will not wreak his vengeance down upon you ... for God's heart is truly but a gentle thing, and is not condemning nor judgmental.

And for all of those of you who cry out loudly, "Yes, we hear God's voice and this is what he says," then listen very carefully, for if you truly hear God's voice which calls out to you then you will truly hear his pleading heart which cries out for tolerance and for understanding.

And all of you will recognize when I say to you, "Let him who will cast the first stone be free of all ill . . . be free of all ill will . . . be free of all guilt . . . and be a purely and righteous person."

And is there one of you who stands upon the earth's plane who can truly look into the eyes of God and say that this person is I . . . and here I am?

A soul will enter into a physical state. A child will live and grow, and breathe within its mother's womb.

And for many reasons . . . many of which are beyond your comprehension . . . sometimes this life emerges for you to see . . . for you to witness. And a child . . . a new child . . . will be born to the earth plane. And sometimes, and however brief this new life may be, a child is born and the universe takes it . . . and takes it to its heart . . . and nurtures it there.

And that you do not see it, nor witness it, or hear its cry or feel its heartbeat . . . will only tell you that you are blind . . . will only tell you that you are deaf.

And yet, we in the spirit world will know that this child is safe and is, truly, born again.

And there is no judgment or condemnation, for God . . . this force which is God . . . which is truly pure and truly understanding . . . will only recognize and accept the decision of the soul to come back to its source.

• • •

Here we have conflict, for Grey Eagle, in saying that all life is sacred, leads me to ask this question: Is aiding an abortion tantamount to an act of murder, or aiding murder? I am somewhat confused, as he also says that it is the soul that makes the choice, and no one else.

And I hear his voice, and I am reminded that the conflict I see is that of earth and universe.

Within our society it is important to have rules, laws, and in all democratic countries our laws are based upon what the majority decides is right. If a country or state decides that abortion is *against the law*, then, because we must live in an ordered society where each man, woman, and child is protected by the law, then we must abide by the law. If as individuals we consider a law to be wrong, harmful, then, respecting our fellow man, we must find a peaceable way to change the law, to alter the mind of the majority if we can, in a democratic fashion, thereby protecting our society from falling apart. Whether abortion is murder or not murder is not the issue I question here. Society has ruled, the law states.

But the rules of the universe are based on much more knowledge than we mortals can possibly envision. Our questions to the universe must seem sometimes so naive, but with our limited knowledge we struggle, and try to learn more of the ways of the spirit world and all of its mysteries. And I hear Grey Eagle's voice again . . . "Those who claim that the aborting of a soul from a physical body destroys that life, do not understand the strength of the soul . . . of the spirit . . . do not understand . . ." And I smile, willing to accept that there is so very much that I do not understand.

I go back and review Grey Eagle's answer once again. I feel his hand on my shoulder, I hear his words, and knowing and trusting his wisdom, accept, realizing how my/our concepts, we who travel this earth, can only guess at the magnitude of God's universe, how as mere mortals, how limited our vision, how limited our concepts. We are children, and as such, understand little, while striving to understand all. But I take heart, for I am a willing student.

Question: Another heated debate in America, as in many parts of the world, regards the issue of homosexuality. Should homosexuality be condoned by society at large as another acceptable way of life?

Answer: And I will say to you again, and yet once again, and I will continue to repeat, and yet once again . . . there are many of you who will hold a holy book in your hand . . . whatever you may call this holy book . . . the Bible, or any other name . . . and you will read the words written therein, and you will take these words to be God's words.

And we hear you call out to us of your love for good and of your love of mankind. And so it is distressing for us to see that for all of you who take God's love to your heart . . . yet still you are blind and do not see that God's love is infinite . . . God's love is whole . . . and God lives, truly, within the heart of each and every one.

And if you will look at your neighbor and despise him or even one small part of him, then you will despise that within him which is God, and you will deny God.

And if you will look at your fellow man and judge him in anger . . . then truly I will say to you, and from my heart, for as surely as God resides in each and every one of us . . . you will judge God and condemn him.

Each man, woman, and child upon the earth plane has a right to be there . . . to live peaceably and in harmony.

Each man, woman, and child has a personality which is individual to that individual, and no man may judge another harshly ... but that he judges God.

For God's place is within the heart of every human soul. And God lives and breathes within the heart of the soul ... and is, indeed, the heart of the soul.

And God's love is all encompassing.

And he will not choose one from another ... nor, yet, say one is better than another. For we are all his children, and he is the heartbeat which allows the soul its survival.

And so if there is one of you who will cast the first stone in condemning or in judgment of another ... judging harshly or cruelly, then I will tell you, truly, that the stone that you will cast, you will cast toward God, and he will feel the pain of it.

• • •

Again I hear Grey Eagle's words, and wonder at the wisdom of them, and at the gentleness with which he teaches.

Something about his answer here reminds me of the Buddhist teachings, and this in turn reminds me of the reason I am asking these questions.

Thinking again, out loud, on the page, I search for truths, for rules, for laws, finding some, but still not ready to make my conclusions. Will I ever be? I ask myself.

I feel the need to ask just one more question, and reaching into the many questions, many writings of Grey Eagle, which may someday become a Book of Questions, my fingers light upon this next, which was asked more than three years ago.

Pulling out the pages, I scan the question, and understand fully, yet not by any means for the first time, how close my guide is to me, how clearly he sees my individual need. For this question is one that is personal to me, applies to someone close to me, dear to me, and my fear for this individual has been great.

Nervous, but knowing I will hear what I need to hear, understanding that I am about to hear a personal truth, I read on.

Question: Grey Eagle, do you have any advice for those people who are striving to recover from alcohol or drug abuse? Many who are striving do not succeed.

Answer: To say the phrase "drug abuse" ... to say the phrase "alcohol abuse" ... drugs, alcohol, are not the issue here.

On your planet, there are many temptations. Some of these temptations you may see as harmful ... and when you refer to these temptations as being harmful, you refer, often, as harmful to the physical self.

There are many temptations which you will consider to be harmless. And, again, you may look at the effect of these things upon your physical self. You will see that there are many things that will not only affect, in an adverse way, the state of your physical body, but they will, also, affect, in an adverse way, the state of your mental well-being and the way you think ... the way you feel ... an outward way.

There are those of you on the earth plane who live in an overindulgent society. Creating this society, each individual takes responsibility, but yet is more than willing to shelve it to the next ... to shelve that responsibility to the next.

And so for each man or woman who takes a bottle and places it to his lips in order that he should drink himself into a state of oblivion for whatever reason he may think he has, each man who does not take up the bottle is just as responsible.

For do you not live side by side? And does not the behavior of one affect the other?

There are many reasons which you will say . . . countless reasons which you say will be the cause of overindulgence in those things that you will see as harmful. But the secret is to look for the root . . . the root cause.

And as I have said before, when you truly look at yourself and you look within yourself to discover the reasons for your own behavior . . . and when you find your behavior lacking in some way, and the outcome is confusion and anxiety . . . destruction . . . you will find that the root cause will be named fear.

I could give you the word "love" . . . and true loving of your fellow man.

I could give you the word "gentleness" . . . in the hope that you will . . . each of you . . . look into your hearts to find that . . . not only for yourself, but for your neighbor.

And I could say these things, that these are truly a remedy for all ills and for all that which ails the individual.

But there will be many of you who will be indifferent to my words and will shrug your shoulders and will say, "But what remedy is that? And can we truly say that to love the drunk will cure him?"

And I will say to you, and truly from my heart, that this is so.

For each soul, before the beginning of its life on the earth plane ... during its life on the earth plane ... and thereafter continuing its life ... craves love ... needs loving ... seeks loving and also to love.

We in the spirit world ... we of the universe ... we watch as humankind slowly destroys itself with its overindulgence.

When I use the words "greed," "avarice," "indifference," you will recognize these words and you will agree with me. But even these things are not the true reasons why many souls writhe in distress, and much of humankind is destroyed.

The root of this is fear ... fear of being still ... fear of recognizing one's own heart ... fear of recognizing one's own soul ...

Fear, which stops the many from daring to look into that mirror, which tells you, truly, who you are ... who you have been ... and who you will be.

You talk of those who are in distress ... those who will fail. And I will tell you, truly, and from my heart, they will only fail if there is a desire deep within them ... buried deep, deep within them ... they will only fail if that desire is to fail.

For each man has a choice, and no other man nor woman can make this choice for them.

But if each one, if every human soul, were to reach out its hand with loving and with gentleness toward its fellow human soul ... then you would know peace, and you would know harmony ... and you would know unity, and you would know wholeness ...

... and you would know you.

• • •

And I hear his words, and I go back, and back, and back again, reading and rereading. For a time I become so engrossed in the answer that I forget the purpose of the question.

My eyes find their way over and over to these words: "And can we truly say that to love the drunk will cure him?"

Reading this, trying to absorb this, I ask Grey Eagle, "Is this really so?" And I hear his reply: "And I will say to you truly and from my heart that this is so."

My thoughts spill out upon the page, for I know that if I am to take you, the reader, on this journey with me, I must hold nothing back.

"But how can this be? That one special person in my life *is* loved, truly loved, by so many, is loved by me. And what of the parents whose children die of drug overdose? Should they now think that if they had loved more, or differently, their children would be alive?" Violently I shake my head, knowing that isn't right.

Do I know Grey Eagle? Do I trust him? The answer is yes. Emphatically, yes. So I must look now to myself. What is it that I'm missing? What is within the words my guide speaks that I do not hear?

I read again, and then once more, and then I see, or begin to see, a clearer picture. The key is love.

Many of us think that loving someone means staying with that person, accepting everything that person does, for isn't this called unconditional love? No matter how much hurt, no matter what pain we inflict on ourselves by staying with, by putting up with, the person, isn't love supposed to be this way, unconditional and total?

I think of all I've learned over the years, of my guide's teachings, and remember Christ's teachings . . . love yourself.

Clear understanding dawns.

Do we not confuse love with self-sacrifice?

Does giving up on your own self, destroying your own self, for someone else's sake . . . does it help anyone?

Does it help you?

I remember my past, my marriage, my relationships. I know that love and self-sacrifice have been all bound up together. And I know that I must separate them, or be always in conflict with myself, always confused.

As a parent, a loving, caring parent, I encouraged my child's independence, knowing that without it she would not grow. There were often times, still are times, when, seeing her make choices which would not be my choices, I hold my breath and pray hard. But I knew that at a certain age, I must let go and trust that, having done my best as a mother, it would be enough.

So saying, I understand fully that if you truly love someone you must allow them to be themselves, whatever it is they want to be. And if, having given as much as you can, to try to be a good influence, that person continues to choose to be a drug addict or a drunk, no matter how it came to be, no matter who or what the initial influence was, well then, we who love them must respect that choice, and allow them their will.

Self-sacrifice is good for no one.

To stay with someone, "just because" because you love them, can often result in more pain, more confusion, more anger, and can be more harmful to all concerned.

And so, heeding Grey Eagle's words, and thinking out loud, and on paper, I know in my heart that which I have known only in my head before, that you can love someone, with all your mind, with all your heart, and with all your soul...you can love, yet still leave, and yet still love. And this, this giving up, of acknowledging other people's right to be, their choice, and still loving them, could be the greatest gift you could give.

Yet once again I seem to have strayed from my purpose. Truths, rules, laws. And yet this self-indulgence, this assumption that you will follow me as I journey, seems to lead me on, and knowing, hoping, that you journey with me still, is of great comfort to me.

Discovery

And so here we are. Having listened to, and pondered upon, many men's words, and listening to my heart, as Grey Eagle would have me do, I am almost ready to draw my conclusions.

Before I do, however, I want to go back to the beginning of this chapter, to the Ten Commandments, and to make some observations, to be sure I have things clear in my mind.

1. You shall have no other gods before me.

2. You shall not make for yourself an idol....

3. You shall not make wrongful use of the name of the Lord your God....

4. Remember the Sabbath day and keep it holy....

5. Honor your father and your mother....

6. You shall not murder (or kill).

7. You shall not commit adultery.

8. You shall not steal.

9. You shall not bear false witness against your neighbor.

10. You shall not covet your neighbor's house, you shall not covet your neighbor's wife, or male or female slave, or ox, or donkey, or anything that belongs to your neighbor.

How did Moses communicate with God? Did he see him? or hear him? How did he see? How did he hear?

When I ask these questions they seem familiar to me, and I realize why. As a Medium, I am asked over and over . . . how do you see? How do you hear?

And while I by no means imply in even the remotest way that I am like Moses, understanding his greatness, the importance of his role in history, even so, just as I am, Moses was a mortal being, and as inspired by God as I believe he was, even so, I must remember his mortality. And no mortal who ever lived is, or was, infallible.

Even Moses, if he were here on this earth now, in our more modern time, might suggest that his/God's Ten Commandments might be a little outdated, perhaps even a little narrow.

Every society needs rules. Rules are for our protection, protection of the individual, and consequently they become protection for the world, for the universe, for the whole.

But as society grows, as we learn and expand, then should our rules change, to allow us growth? We most of us obviously think so, for in all free and forward-thinking countries, the legal systems are reviewed and changed from time to time, as they should be.

So, continuing, thinking out loud on the page, trying if I can to take you with me on this journey, I look again.

Moses said:

I. *You shall have no other gods before me.* And thinking out loud, and on the page, I wonder, how is it possible to put other gods before, for is God not everything, all things? Is God not light . . . light?

2. *You shall not make for yourself an idol.* As I ponder this, I feel Grey Eagle draw close to me, not to give *his* answer, but to encourage me to find my own. My thoughts then, as I write them, I express to him. . . . Ha! Would not a mirror image be all you would see? A reflection of your own image? For to *create* an idol would only result in an image of your own needs.

3. *You shall not make wrongful use of the name of the Lord your God.* My thoughts, instant here . . . but surely, to disparage any name, of any man or woman, to have that name upon your lips in a disrespectful way, is to disrespect God and all Man. Therefore, you disrespect yourself.

4. *Remember the Sabbath day and keep it holy.* This reminds me of a story my close friend Joan told me. She came out into her garden. The day was warm and sunny, a perfect spring day. She noticed the old gentleman who lived opposite, also in his garden, and she waved, and called out, "Isn't it a beautiful day?" He smiled and waved back, replying, "Every day is beautiful—it just happens that the sun is shining today!" My thoughts are his thoughts . . . each day is a "holy" day. And each day must be treasured, for if this is not done, if all days, and all nights, are not looked upon as special, then how will we recognize the earth's beauty, which is of God, given as a gift to us?

5. *Honor your father and your mother.* My thoughts here are simple. I don't believe that a man's position, status, uniform, automatically entitles him to honor and respect. I feel that it is his behavior which determines this. In our society today, it is unfortunate that we see so much abuse, and the abuse of parents against their children, so I would

say ... only when you know a person can you honor them, or not.

6. *You shall not murder (or kill).* I sigh, and shake my head in despair. Grey Eagle's hand is on my shoulder, understanding my pain. My thoughts go to the struggle of our earth, our planet, to the wars, where in order to defend what we believe, to defend our rights, the right to be, it has been necessary to kill. To kill in order to protect, to defend, not just ourselves, but our families, our society, is one thing. However, to put your will forcibly upon any man or woman is to deny him or her the freedom to be. And if you take away another's rights, you deny yourself all right to be.

7. *You shall not commit adultery.* Adultery is the act of breaking a vow, of breaking a promise. Whether the act of breaking that vow is discovered or not by a partner, my thoughts here are easy ones. Surely, to commit any act which you know in your heart could cause pain to another, to *deliberately* maim or injure, whether emotionally or physically, is an act of pure selfishness. And the eyes of the spirit world will look down, not in judgment, but with sadness, recognizing the violation of that vow. For whatever pain you deliberately inflict on another will be brought back to you tenfold. *This is the law of the universe.* What is given out must be taken back.

8. *You shall not steal.* My thoughts go back to those ancient times, the time of Moses. History tells us of the poverty which ordinary people had to suffer. And then, even in our modern time, there is such great poverty in the world. Therefore, knowing my God to be a gentle and loving God, my thoughts are these.... And who is to say that the

man who steals a loaf of bread to feed his starving children is a man condemned by God?

9. *You shall not bear false witness against your neighbor.* And nodding my agreement, even so, I must take it further. For Grey Eagle has taught me, and my thoughts are clear.... However it matters that you should lie to another, it matters more that you should lie to yourself.

10. *You shall not covet your neighbor's house . . . or wife, or male or female slave, or ox, or donkey, or anything that belongs to your neighbor.* We are taught in the Bible that a man's material possessions are valueless, so although I understand and agree with the sentiment of this rule, I wonder that Moses did not take the sentiment further. I remember then, as I think this, that his people were simple and mainly uneducated. My thoughts are broader, wider. The man or woman who craves another man's belongings is a man to be pitied. For he or she does not know that the only true possession, the only one of any value, is his or her own self.

Now these thoughts are mine. And although you journey with me, and I am mindful of your company, and glad of it, I do not expect that you should agree with me. It would only please me if you take a little of what I say, if in your heart, as you read my thoughts, you recognize a small truth.

Having come this far, and yet still placing my thoughts upon the page, I must go back to the beginning of this chapter, to remind myself once again, and for the final time, the purpose of the exercise.

I was looking for Rules. And along the way I began looking for Laws, and Truths.

Laws . . . Rules . . . Truths . . . is there a difference? Is a rule different from a law? I reach for the dictionaries. The *Concise Oxford* and the *Collins National.*

Law

A Rule enacted, or customary, in a community, prohibiting certain actions, and *enforced by penalties.*
A rule established *by authority.*
A body of rules, the practice of which is *authorized* by a community or state.
A divine commandment, as expressed in the Bible. *The Law of Moses.*

Rule

A *principle* to which an *action conforms.*
Prevailing custom or standard.
Code of discipline.

Truth

Honesty.
Religious tenet, based on *revelation.*
Constancy.

So, yes, a rule is different from a law.

Many of you may think me a little slow for asking this question at all, but, my thoughts on paper, I have to question everything, and I simply wasn't sure.

But having almost completed the exercise, I am becoming sure of, or at least clear of, the fact that we, or I at least, do need rules, and truths, as guides, a steering implement, in order that I can more easily follow my chosen path. I realize, and am happy that, throughout my life, my future, these rules, these truths, may change. They are not set in stone. I realize too that it is I who may change them, as my needs, my growth, my understanding, expands.

Laws, however, the Laws of the Universe, obviously in place because the universe needs, these Laws are formed as the universe is formed, change as the universe changes, and only God dictates these changes. Only God knows the all-encompassing needs of his creation.

These are my thoughts, placed on the page, so that you may share them, share the process, and take them or discard them if you will.

And so I conclude...

Laws of the Universe

1. Each being is responsible for... *owns*... its own soul.
2. One man is the whole, which is one man, which is the whole, which is... the circle of light, unbroken.
3. What is given out must be taken back, must return to its source.
4. There is not one being... one living thing, that does not have God at its center, at the heart of it. No man, woman, or child is exempt from this Law.
5. All things, each being, all things living, return to the source, which is God, is light.
6. Each soul has choice, and will exercise that choice, and has, by its very existence, exercised its choice.
7. Each soul is its own Law.

Rules

1. Honor yourself, respect yourself, love yourself... from this will come respect, love, and honor of all which is of the earth, which is of God.

2. Tolerance . . . first of yourself, and then for all humankind.
3. Kindness, benevolence, for yourself . . . through which you will learn to open your heart to others.
4. Gentleness . . . given this first to your own heart, which will be healed, which will then reach out to all hearts.
5. Humility . . . from which comes all spiritual growth.
6. Compassion . . . for in giving love and sympathy to another's distress or suffering, great understanding of your own soul will be your discovery.
7. Grace . . . live by these rules, with grace, with courteous goodwill, and receive the unmerited favor of God.

Truths

I. I do not see God as a dictator . . . rather, I see a benevolent force.
2. Prayer is not just the experience of being in the presence of God. More, prayer is one way to acknowledge that ever-present God force.
3. God does not forget us, even though he is all too frequently forgotten.
4. You must have leadership of your own soul.
5. Dying is a birthing experience.
6. Miracles are not just experiences we read in the Bible. Miracles happen in our world today, and every day.
7. The truth is that which touches your heart, and echoes within the heart of your soul, which is God.

In ending this chapter, I once again reach for my Bible, this time the New Testament. And I do not quote these words because they are other men's words, but simply because they express sentiments I strive hard, while failing, to live by.

Matthew 7:1–5

Do not judge, so that you may not be judged.

For with the judgment you make, you will be judged.

And the measure you will give, will be the measure you get.

Why do you see the speck in your neighbor's eye, but do not notice the log in your own eye?

Or, how can you say to your neighbor, "Let me take the speck out of your eye," while the log is in your own eye?

You hypocrite. First take the log out of your own eye, and then you will see clearly to take the speck out of your neighbor's eye.

Matthew 25:35–36, 40

And Jesus, talking about the Great Judgment, says ...

For I was hungry, and you gave me food.

I was thirsty, and you gave me something to drink.

I was a stranger, and you welcomed me.

I was naked, and you gave me clothing.

I was sick, and you took care of me.

I was in prison, and you visited me....

Truly, I tell you, just as you did this to one of the least of these who are my brothers, you did this to me.

Question: Grey Eagle, can we look forward to a more pervasive sense of spirituality in this world?

Answer: Each man, woman, and child ... each being ... will have its own choice.

For, no matter how naive you may seem to be ... for no matter how naive your neighbor ... each being has, within it, the soul ... the knowing self.

Each being has, within it, the knowledge to choose.

And the way that you should live ... the way that you should grow ... the way that you should be ... is your choice.

And if only you would listen to the wind which tells you this story ...

And if only you would gaze to the heavens and see our faces smiling down upon you ...

And if only you were to touch the earth and, knowing that its roots ... that your roots ... go deep within it, but that you can grow as high toward the sky as it is possible ...

If only you would know these things ...

If only you would listen to your knowing self, then peace would not just be for the individual but for all of humankind.

And then peace would not just be for the individual ... it would not just be for all humankind, but the universe would grow ...

And the universe would shake a little with the anticipation of such a thing.

Journey to the Mountain

"I HEARD IT CALL TO ME"

Many things have happened in the two years since I wrote *The Eagle and the Rose*. The first was that my mother "died." My last contact with her had been five years previous to her death. I had just finished the last chapter of the book, "The Girl," and although the writing was painful, as many memories of my childhood surfaced in my head, many I had pushed down into my subconscious over the years, it was also a great cleansing, a way of facing up to who I really am. In remembering, many questions were answered, questions like: Why was I so self-conscious? Why was I lacking in self-worth? Why did I need to prove self-worth? Why was I so sensitive? Why was I so afraid?

Exploring my life, and finding those questions, and being able, for the most part, to answer them was very beneficial to me. However, I was left with one question, one burning question, I was unable to find an answer to, and as my father had died some several years earlier, I knew that only my mother would be able to answer.

My question, childlike in its simplicity and naïveté, was: Why did my parents treat me the way they did?

What is it that can drive a person to behave so badly, so meanly, toward a small child, not just on an odd occasion, but on an almost constant daily, yearly basis ... spanning years, from childhood into adulthood? What is it that drives a person to abusive behavior toward a small child, who is, after all, just a small child?

What was it that drove my parents to behave this way toward me?

In the past I had believed that it must be my fault. There were four of us, four sisters, and I was the skinny one, the one who wore glasses, the one who cried all the time, ugly, unshapely, a crybaby. These were some of the reasons why I had grown up believing that in so many ways, I was an inadequate human being.

The chapter written, my tears dry on the page, but still flowing from my heart, I approached my mother, not aggressively, not in any challenging way, but simply looking for answers, and a way forward in our relationship. And so I asked her why.

Her answer: "It was your father, not me, not me. You can't blame me."

I wasn't looking to blame, just to understand, and told her so.

"Your father, it was all his fault, not mine."

And I was sad. Quietly, trying to be gentle, maybe failing, I reminded her of some of the cruel things she had done, things that had occurred when my father was away, "things you did," I said, "which had nothing to do with anyone but you and me."

She gasped, completely taken back by the things I had remembered, then she screamed, "You don't know what I had done to me. Knifed in the back! You and everyone else, all my life, people knifed me in the back."

Was it at this point that I gave up, or later when I thought things over? I don't know. All I was hearing was self-pity, and I knew the moment I recognized that fact that I would never have my question answered, for the truth was that my mother had, all her life, been so enraged and wrapped up in her own misery that she had not even been aware of mine and the part she had played in it.

It was five years later that she died. We had not communicated in all that time, for there was nothing to say, and when my sister called to give me the news, I felt nothing. The entire day I wondered why, why I felt no sense of loss, or even sadness. "I am not a callous person," I reasoned, "and I am a caring person." Then it came to me. I had lost my mother five years ago. I had "let go" of my hopes and dreams that my mother might be a real mother to me. And I had cried, I had grieved my loss, then.

Two days later I left for America, there to continue my spiritual journey.

It was late in March 1995, just a few weeks before *The Eagle and the Rose* was published. We—my agent and friend Joni Evans and I—had flown to Phoenix, had rented a car, and had made our way to the mountain.

If you remember, I recounted at the beginning of this book my first visit to the mountain with my friend Lynn. I spoke to you then Grey Eagle's words: "Not here, not now, this is not the time, but you will come back."

Well, now I was back, and I knew that now was the time.

We got out of the car and began to walk around the mountain, looking now for a break in the fence which had held me back over a year ago.

Joni, excited, began to walk ahead of me, eager to hurry things along—so eager, so excited, she ignored the car parked at the side of the road up ahead of us, and as she passed it, she did not notice the two women inside.

"Come on," she called from time to time, looking back at my slower progress. "Come on, come on."

But I was in no hurry. I knew, my instinct told me, that I was in the right place, at the right time, and I could afford the time to take notice.

I looked at the sky, so blue and clear, and noticed how still everything seemed. I noticed the majesty of the mountain, heard it call to me, knew it was waiting, that it would wait for me. And I noticed the car, and as I approached, noticed the two women, one older, mother and daughter, I knew. And I smiled, knowing that their presence there was no accident, that without even knowing it, they were waiting too. Waiting for me.

Steadily I approached the car. The windows were down, and the older of the two women was resting her arm on the edge. I smiled and stopped, and said what a beautiful day it was, and didn't the mountain look perfect. The woman smiled back, agreeing that although it was hot, indeed the day and the mountain were beautiful.

"Have you come far?" I inquired.

"My daughter has come from California," she said, "but I'm local. We come here every year at this time. This was my husband's favorite place. When he died we scattered his ashes on the mountain. It was what he wanted to do, and so we come here once a year for him."

As she said this last she began to cry a little, and I reached forward and gently placed my hand on her arm. "I don't know if you believe in survival after death," I said, "but I do. And I believe that your husband is here with you now, that he is sharing these precious moments with you, and that he has survived death, and is unharmed." Then, a smile on my face, I said, "I believe, too, that he has probably walked up and explored the mountain many times since he died."

"Do you really believe that?" the woman in the car asked. "You know," she mused, "it was his most favorite thing to do, to explore the mountain. We have so many photographs he took. Could it really be possible that he is here with us now?"

Gently I squeezed her arm. "I would bet on it," I said.

Again, tears sprang to her eyes, and she said, "Oh, if only I could believe that."

Now I could hear my friend Joni calling. She had found the break in the fence I knew would be there. "Come on," she called. "What are you doing? Come on, come on, we're almost there."

I knew it was time to go, but I had one more thing to say before I took my leave. I looked into her eyes, this stranger who had been waiting, and said, "Loss is a terrible thing, and we all pray that it doesn't happen to us, that we might be the first to go. Life becomes hard, almost impossible sometimes, for to live without our loved ones around us, on this earth, is a great hardship." I paused, then continued, "There is a book I think you should read, which I feel will help you greatly. It's called *The Eagle and the Rose*. The author's name is Rosemary Altea." As I said this, the daughter handed me a pen and paper, and I wrote it down for them. "Read it," I said softly. "I pray that it gives you hope, and helps the pain a little."

There were no goodbyes, and as I moved off and made my way to where my friend was impatiently waiting, I smiled, and thought how fitting it was that the first time I was able to recommend that someone should read my book, it would be as I stood at the foot of the mountain, our mountain, Grey Eagle's and mine.

And there are those of you who may not believe. And there are those of you who, understanding the ways of the Native Americans, sensing the strength of the eagle, will acknowledge and accept my truth.

We began to climb the mountain. I was in the lead, and Joni, the fitter of the two of us by far, began to tire.

"How much farther?" I heard her say behind me, panting a little, and out of breath.

"We have to go just a bit farther," I said, pausing, allowing her to catch up. I pointed ahead. "Way up there," I said, "is a large flat rock. We have to make our way to that."

"But how do you . . . ?" Her sentence was never finished; she had realized quickly that it was a dumb question to ask.

I stood up straight and, laughing, began to stride up the mountain once more, picking my way through rocks and brush with ease, my purpose clear. Energy coursed its way through me, not just my body, my mind too. I felt strong, invincible, as I absorbed the power, and my spirit soared.

The mountain, the mountain, and I could hear its voice as it welcomed me home.

Finally we came to the rock, large and flat, as Grey Eagle had described, and I motioned to Joni that this was where we would sit. Grateful to rest, she sank down onto the rock, and sitting down next to her, I was aware of the silence, of the stillness, of the sun warming my arms, my face, and as I looked to the mountain, high up to the top, I felt an anticipation, a silent knowing, filling the air.

"Grey Eagle is here, but not alone," I thought, and instantly heard his acknowledgment, then his hand on my shoulder. . . .

"Listen," he said. "Listen. There are many here, and I have a story to tell, a story for you both to hear."

I nodded, knowing, understanding, that I must recount to Joni all that Grey Eagle now would say.

As my guide had done with me, I now placed my hand on Joni's shoulder, and just as he had, now I said to her, "Listen, listen. There are many here, and Grey Eagle has a story to tell us. . . ."

"And there were women and children. And the men, those of our people who were left, brought them here to the mountain, where we hid from the white eye. And the soldiers came, and searched for us, finding only a few, and we were killed.

"And the women fought, and yes, even our children. Those who were old enough to lift but one small stone. And we fought, and ran, and hid, and fought. But we could not fight starvation. And the women and children, those who were left, lay with the men, fought with the men, starved and were killed with the men.

"And many died. Their bodies lay on the mountain. And the blood of my people ran down the mountain, flowed like many rivers. And the blood soaked into the rock, and the rain came, and cleansed the mountain, washed away the blood of my people.

"Many Apache have stayed on the mountain, walked the mountain, their spirits echo. Their voices silent, as they wait.

"Now they wake, but not from sleep, yet from that time of waiting. And they rise up, and all together, and in unity, as all people must, and calling out to each other, know that now we celebrate. For this is our beginning, our new beginning"—and this last said to me—"and you have brought us our beginning."

My guide, having ended his story, and now standing before me, turned and waved his hand toward the mountain. "Look now," he said to me. "Look now, and you will see the rising up of my people. Listen now, and you will hear them call, and you will hear the drums, and the singing, and the laughter, as they dance, and as they celebrate their new beginning."

And as Grey Eagle spoke these words, and as I quietly recounted to Joni all he said, I looked, and saw, and saw many people rising up from the ground. And the mountain was covered. And I listened and heard. And the drums beat loud, and the singing grew louder, and I watched the people as they danced.

I heard then a small startled cry from my friend, and turned to her. She whispered, "Is this real? Is this really so? I can hear drums, I can hear people calling out, and singing, I can hear singing." And I watched as tears fell from her eyes, and she stood with her head bent low, in silent prayer, grateful to have been chosen to share this experience.

I looked to my guide, my own cheeks wet with tears, and he spoke again, and again, waving his arms wide toward the mountain.

"And these you see are not just my people, not all Apache, but people of many nations, many lands around the world. And we unite, and are one people, for we are of spirit, are spirit, even as you who are of the earth are spirit. And we who have 'died' have so small a voice, a voice which, until now, has been rarely heard, often ignored, through ignorance and doubt, and yes, often through fear."

And as Grey Eagle spoke, the drums grew louder, and a chanting, a ritual chanting, began, and it was as if I now stood in the heart of the mountain as my guide spoke again, this time just to me.

"And you have been our voice, and yet will continue to be our voice. The voice of all who have 'died' who would wish to have a voice." And then, said gently, lovingly, "And this is not an easy task, but one you chose. And all whose hearts you touch will hear our voice, and know that, yes, we live.

"And we who are spirit, and of the spirit world, we who are light, will call to you, you who are spirit, and of the earth world, you who are light, and we will be united once more.

"And we are spirit. And we are proud. All here who have risen from the mountain.

"And my name is Grey Eagle, and I am Apache. And I am spirit . . . and I am proud . . . Proud Spirit."

I began my descent from the mountain, Joni, silent, following behind. It was as we reached the bottom that I heard him call. I looked up, high, high in the sky. Joni, grabbing hold of me, said, "See him, can you see him?" And I laughed, and laughed and laughed, as I stood with my friend and watched. He had come from behind the mountain, soaring high in the sky, then lower and lower, and now circling over our heads, before soaring again, up, up, high, and over the mountain again. He was beautiful, wingspan wide, the tips gold, catching the sun. And back he came, back, and flying over head, and then he flew high . . . the eagle.

THE JOURNEY CONTINUES

The next time I visited the mountain I was with my friend and editor Joann Davis. Phoenix was one of the cities we were in promoting *The Eagle and the Rose*, which had just hit the *New York Times* best-seller list, a thrilling and momentous occasion.

We had taken the morning off, had hired a jeep and a driver, Lenny, a wonderful man, a cowboy who, he told us, was married to a great lady, a Native American woman, and we had found our way back to the mountain.

As we sat on the rock, the same rock that I had sat on with Joni, again Grey Eagle spoke to us both, again he spoke just to me, telling us that this was just the beginning. And again he said, "Now listen, listen, and hear the sound of the drums, and hear us call to each other as we celebrate, as we rise up, for our time, the time when the voice of the spirit world will be truly heard, that time has come."

Already I could hear them. And again I saw them on the mountain, and again I heard their drums. And I looked, and saw that Joann had heard it too. Then, "I can hear a sound, like sticks, sticks, rapped against each other. A clacking sound. And drums, and voices calling. Can you hear it?" she asked, incredulously.

And I held her hand and nodded, saying yes, but knowing, as I had known with Joni, that I could hear more, see more, but thrilled that my friend was able to experience some of it. And again I laughed out loud, joyful, as the eagle again came over the mountain.

And there are those of you who may not believe. And there are those of you who, understanding the ways of the native Americans, sensing the strength of the eagle, will acknowledge and accept my truth, my story, which I sense, I know, at least as far as this book goes, is coming to a close.

✻   ✻   ✻

It is no coincidence that as I have been writing this chapter I am in Phoenix, having arrived here just a few days ago, to give my first workshop in America, a healing workshop. It seems only appropriate that the story of the mountain should be written here. I had not planned that it should be this way, but perhaps Grey Eagle had.

Yesterday... but wait. I'm moving too quickly, for first, before I tell you of yesterday, I must tell you that it was only two months ago that I was here. This time to give a lecture. Samantha and my love came with me, and, of course, we visited the mountain. This time there were no drums, nor was there any singing, not that they could hear. This time was different, for I had brought them here in the hope that each of them, for different reasons, would have a healing experience. And as I stood with them, the three of us facing the mountain, I placed my hands upon them, and looking to my guide, and looking to Christ, and reaching out with all my heart to my God, I asked that the two people I loved most should receive the gift of healing.

Neither knew, nor have I told them yet. They will learn of this only when they read it from this page.

Samantha was suffering and in pain. A broken relationship, and like all mothers, I needed to see her healed. Knowing she is strong, her mother's child, I know she will be well in time.

My love... my love... well, where should I begin?

THE WOMAN

It was Christmas. She was in Vermont, perhaps the most beautiful place to be at such a time. All was snow, and snowing, and as she looked out the window on Christmas morning, she felt that she was in some wonderful winter wonderland. A land of fairy tales, of "happy-every-afters," where rosy-cheeked children danced and played, a land of elves and pixies and Santa Claus ... and magic.

Just being here was enough, was her Christmas gift. She was with friends, with her daughter, and all was good.

It was not a time to reflect on the past, nor did she. Had she done so she might have remembered her childhood, the pain and sadness. She certainly would have remembered the confusions of her teenage years, then her marriage, which began and ended badly. But now was not the time for those things. All that was past, and in the past, for she had conquered the miseries of her life, and was now at peace, happy in her work, successful, thriving, and best of all, content.

"Oh dear Lord," she murmured, as she looked out at the snow-laden trees, at the ground, deep in snow, pure and clean, awaiting the first signs of life, a footprint or two, perhaps. "Oh dear Lord, I thank you for this year, for the peace you have helped me find, and for this day, which is your day." And smiling and happy, she made her way downstairs to breakfast.

How innocent we are. How innocent she was, little realizing that within a few short hours her life would take a new turn, would be changed forever.

She wasn't looking for love. Indeed, if anyone had told her she was about to find it, she would have steeled herself against it. It had been four years since she had dated. Not because she hadn't been asked. Oh no. There had been many offers, but she had refused them all. Relationships were too complicated, she didn't have time, didn't want to make time. She was very happy, truly happy, as she was.

The day had been wonderful. She and her daughter had had a great time with their friends, and now they were all seated at the home of the Fergusons, who had invited them all, several weeks earlier, to join them for Christmas dinner.

It was as dessert was being served that he came, and his arrival was heralded by the dog, Maggie, who went crazy as soon as she saw him, instantly lying on her back, legs in the air, crying and crying with joy, ecstatic to see him.

The woman, her back to this scene, half turned in her chair, amused by the dog's antics, but only mildly interested in the man.

They were introduced, and he was seated at the top end of the table, quite close to her, next to the hostess, who, like the dog, seemed to adore him.

"He's having a really tough time, going through a terrible divorce, and he's such a wonderful person," the hostess whispered intimately to the woman, some ten minutes later. But the woman, uninterested, merely nodded, and feeling the need to escape more gossip, she rose and went to stand by the fire.

It had been a good day, and now she was ready to leave, to go home, back to her friend's house. She felt skittish, like a nervous colt, but for no reason she could think of. Something, she wasn't sure what, had unnerved her, and she wanted to go.

It was as she sat back down at the table that he spoke to her directly for the first time, and as she answered him, he looked right at her, and for one brief second their eyes locked, and held, and then she looked away. She was not embarrassed, nor was she shy, just a little shocked by the intensity of the moment, and when, an hour later, he took his leave, she was not surprised that he came to her last to say goodbye, and she was only a little amused that he took her hand and expressed a wish that he might see her again.

She gave him no more thought until the next afternoon, when he telephoned to ask her out to dinner. And with no thought whatsoever, she said yes.

It was the 27th of December when they had their first date, and over the next few days, before she left for New York, they spent a great deal of time together. It was, of course, inconceivable that they would become anything other than friends. Their lives were worlds apart. He was a stockbroker; his business was in

Vermont. She, well, she was a traveler, had rarely been in the same country for more than a few weeks at a time over the last eighteen months. The idea of a relationship developing was nonsense, and they both knew it. But when they held hands, they both knew that something special was happening too. There was between them a gentleness, a quietness, and an inevitability.

It was in those first few days that the woman discovered, through the Fergursons, that Jim was an alcoholic, and listening to them as again they told her what a wonderful man he was, how gentle and kind, she saw only his pain, only his sensitivity, and her heart went out to him.

And it was only two days later, as they sat at the top of the mountain where he had taken her to show her where he skied, that she held his hand and gently but firmly told him that no decent woman would want a relationship with a drunk, with a man who held a bottle in his hands.

She was used to pain. Pain had been her life, and was now her work, but being used to seeing it did not make it easier when she saw his pain as she spoke these words to him.

Three more days passed, and through those days they spent many hours together, and small seeds took root, small seeds of love.

She left for New York, then went on to England, where she stayed a week or so before going on to Australia and New Zealand.

They had agreed to stay friends, neither willing to commit to the idea that there was a chance for something more. But the phone calls increased, and pretty soon they were speaking to each other every day, and their romance blossomed.

He was sober now, he told her, was sorting out his life, and had stopped drinking.

She, on hearing this, not quite believing, only hoped that this was so, and remembering his words to her as they had spoken on the telephone those weeks ago in Vermont, on New Year's Eve, she placed her trust in God.

"And I truly believe that God has sent you to me," he had said, and as she heard these words, knowing he was right, she had thought, "And I believe that God has sent you to me also."

When, in January, he asked her to spend some time with him in Vermont, to come to the mountain, where she could relax and find some quiet time after the exhaustion of her constant traveling, she agreed to spend the whole of February, knowing that this was to be the test of their relationship.

As the time drew closer, even though they had spent many hours talking on the telephone, both had second thoughts.

"What if she's ugly?" he thought, not quite remembering what she looked like. "Oh God, what if she's fat?"

And she wondered, "What if I don't like him? What if he's still drinking? What if, what if, what if...?"

He was waiting outside when the car arrived, and she had seen him before he saw her. It was as the car pulled to a stop, and he saw her face at the window looking out at him, he told her later, that he knew for certain that he was in love with her. And as he held her in his arms, she knew she had been right to come, that she loved him, even though she was not yet truly "in love" with him.

It was an idyllic month, perhaps, aside from the time her daughter was born, the happiest time of her life. He bought her roses, each week he bought her three pink roses, and placing them by her bedside, he would look from them to her and back again.

"I can't decide," he said, smiling down at her one morning, "which is more beautiful, the roses, or you." And leaning down, he placed a kiss on her lips and murmured softly, "I think you are."

And she would gently stroke his face, his hair, and think to herself as she wound her arms around him how handsome he was, how wonderful.

Many times during that first month, she would wake in the

night, open her eyes, and find him staring down at her lovingly, wonderingly, and she would smile up at him, and reaching out, would softly stroke his cheek, his lips, before falling back to sleep.

One day he came home with candles, and placing them, too, by her bedside, next to her roses, said, "I want us always to light a candle before we go to sleep, so that if I wake in the night I will be able to see your face in the candlelight."

The days went by slowly, and as they played in the snow, and as she cooked for him, and as he took her out for candlelit dinners, and as they lay in their bed and talked for hours and hours into the night, night after night, so, slowly, she began to fall in love with him. And he, already in love, admitting his love, would ask her, "Say you're in love with me, just say you're in love."

And he would tease her lovingly, and they would laugh together, she shaking her head, not ready yet to say she was in love, knowing it was just a matter of time.

Then, time running out, their time together came to an end, for she had to return to England, and to business.

He held her tenderly as they said goodbye, and tasted the tears on her cheeks as he kissed her face. "I love you, I am in love with you," he whispered fiercely, and he held her close as she whispered back, "I love you too."

Was heaven like this? she wondered, sometime later, as the plane soared high up into the sky. But she was not thinking of the clouds or the sky, or even the setting sun, but of his arms, Jim's arms, and of the month she had just spent with him.

And he had been drunk only three times.

This time she was away for just a month. Through all of March they talked each day on the phone, and they would tell each other of their lives, of their wants and needs, and hopes, and occasionally they would talk about his drinking. He would assure her that he was working on it, going to AA meetings, getting help, and she, not quite believing, but believing in their love, would remember his words . . . "And God has sent you to me." And knowing this to be true, and with great faith in God, she continued to hope, and to pray.

At the end of March, the woman came back to America, and although she traveled quite a bit throughout the country, still she spent a lot of time with Jim in Vermont.

Their love grown deeper now, she finally said the words he wanted to hear. "I am in love with you," she softly said, and as he kissed her, drew her close, so softly now, he said in gentle tones, "I know you are, and I am in love with you."

If he was drinking now she did not see it, nor did his friends, nor did those people who had, for years, known him only as "an alcoholic." And all they saw, and all they said they saw, was two people with a special love. And this was what it was.

As April ended, so too, did winter. The snow finally disappeared, and buds and birds and bees all spoke of spring, and May. May was her favorite month, the month of her birth. Smiling, she recalled Jim's words to her when asking when her birthday was. "No, no, don't tell me, let me guess," he laughed. "I think, I think," he mused, "you must have been born in May, the most beautiful month of the year. You could not possibly have been born at any other time." He'd said it simply, lovingly, meaning every word.

The eve of her birthday arrived. Friends had traveled from New York, a four-hour drive, to be with her, and they all planned to have dinner at a special restaurant that night. They were to meet at the restaurant at eight o'clock.

It was an exciting time. The woman's daughter had arrived from England to be with her mother, and Jim's sister and brother-in-law had also come for the weekend and were joining them for dinner.

They were ready early, she excited to see her friends again, pleased to be meeting Jim's family for the first time, and it was only as they stood to leave for the restaurant that she noticed.

Why was he standing with his eyes closed? Why did he seem to be swaying a little?

"Jim?" she cried, alarmed, afraid that he was sick. "Jim, darling," now crossing the room to him, "are you okay? You look terrible."

He opened his eyes, but not fully, he couldn't, and she realized with shocking force that he was well and truly drunk. So drunk he could hardly stand.

Why hadn't she seen it? How come she hadn't noticed it sooner?

His sister, concerned, thinking as she had that he must be sick, put her arms around him.

"Jimmy, Jimmy, tell us what's wrong, darling. Tell us what's wrong."

How can she not see? How can she not know? These thoughts raced through the woman's head, and looking at her love, she felt sick.

They didn't go to dinner, and as all good partners are supposed to do, she lied to her friends about the reasons.

She lay in her bed crying well into the night. He, oblivious to her pain, lay next to her in a drunken stupor.

Morning finally came. May 19. Her birthday. She woke, her eyes so swollen with crying she could hardly open them. He stirred, woke, and crept out of bed, thinking she was still asleep. He washed and dressed, and went off to an AA meeting, shame and guilt driving him there.

When he came home she was cooking eggs for breakfast. It was early, but there was a lot to do, as they had invited more than thirty people to her birthday party, and she couldn't let them down.

How she got through it she didn't know. He hadn't even wished her a happy birthday, she thought, but then how could he—he would have choked on the words, knowing, surely knowing, that her heart had begun to break.

He swore it would never happen again, that he would get help,

255

that he needed help, and for a time he went spasmodically to meetings.

She, in turn, began to read, began to learn a little about the thing they call a disease. She began, too, to try to talk to him about it, but each time she tried he became more defensive, and then, eventually, as the drinking progressed, becoming worse and worse, he became aggressive, mean, and nasty.

The times he felt remorse were fewer and fewer, these feelings now replaced by anger, directed more and more at her. He began to criticize her, often in front of others, and he would lose his temper over the smallest thing.

When she had to travel, she would call him from her hotel room in the mornings, when she knew he would be sober. The evenings, when she was on her own, well, they were her time to cry.

It was not all bad. Between the times, those days when he was not drunk, or angry, or frustrated, those good days, which were becoming fewer, on those days he was loving, and he was gentle, and they laughed and shared and loved, but less and less, for each time she reached to put her arms about him she would fear the smell of alcohol. And each time he took a drink, he would avoid her arms, avoid her love. And each time he took a drink, each time she saw him drunk, she would look at him and know his pain, and feel his pain, knowing that he, in turn, would do anything, lie and cheat, deny and deny, do anything so as not to see her pain, to face her pain.

How long could she take this? How much time would pass before she said, "Enough"? What was she waiting for—some miracle, some wonderful, incredible miracle, that would put this right? She didn't know, and for the first time in a very long time, she felt that she had been deserted. For no matter how she asked, and no matter how she tried, there did not seem to be an answer to her pleading questions.

She knew she must not be an enabler, someone he could use, and abuse. Realizing that if she stayed that's what she would become, she left, but after only three days, feeling that he needed her, she returned.

He became more angry, yelled and stormed, and stormed and drank. And drank . . . and drank.

Rarely getting drunk now, a master of cunning and manipulation in his drinking, he thought to deceive her, knowing she was not deceived, but trying anyway. Truly an alcoholic.

And now September was drawing to a close. Nine months since the beginning, a lifetime.

She loved him, was in love with him, and he, hard as it was to believe, he loved her too, was truly, deeply, in love with her. Of this she had no doubt.

And knowing this, she called out to God, knowing that God had brought her to him, this man she loved. She heard a voice, a voice she knew well, and trusted, had trusted for many years. And softly, and always softly, she heard his voice, as if carried on the wind . . . "Trust, little one, trust."

She called again to God, not asking for a cure, not asking for a miracle, but asking now, "What can I learn from this? How can I grow from this? How strong can I become?"

Another trip, more work, more travel, and this time back to Arizona. The relief of leaving was great, leaving the lies and the uncertainties that come with living with an alcoholic. The pain of leaving was also great, for the woman knew that her love would be in pain without her.

She called him when she arrived, but it was around nine in the evening for him, and he was drunk, striving to sound sober, and so she did not call him again for several days. When he eventually called her, it was the same pretense, and so although they spoke, neither really listened, or heard the other's heart.

257

* * *

It is no coincidence that I began writing this chapter in Phoenix. I had not planned that it should be this way, but perhaps Grey Eagle had.

Yesterday... and now I will tell you of yesterday.... yesterday I went again to the mountain, hoping to find hope. I climbed up to my special rock, my friend Joann and my daughter, Samantha, walking with me, just behind. For a while we all sat together and watched as the sun rose up, its rays reaching deep into the crevices of the rock, to places we could not see. Then I asked them both if they would leave me by myself for a while, which they did.

I sat, quite still, Grey Eagle by my side. I looked to him, to Christ, and I looked to God. Thoughts of Jim ran through my mind, and I the "girl," and I the "she" that I have been writing about, and I the "woman," grown, struggling to grow more... and I looked to myself.

No answers came, nor did I truly expect them, but as I sat and listened, and as I looked to my own self, I heard the heartbeat of my soul, I saw my broken heart, and then, with greater clarity than I had had before, I saw my love, my Jim. And he was aged, and bent, and very fragile, and in that moment of seeing, I knew true pity, an emotion I had thought I knew, thought I had experienced before, but never before with such depth, such feeling. I saw him clearly, and pitied that he could not, would not, see himself. See the man he really is, strong, vital, gentle, wonderful. I pitied that, with such little self-esteem, such lack of self-worth, his one aim in life was that he stay in control, keep his world in order, be in control. This need for control was so at odds with the fact that his life was utterly controlled by alcohol.

And will he despise her for her pity of him, refusing to see her love? And will he despise himself more? And will it be enough to make him change, or will he turn away from truth, close his eyes to their pain, and destroy them both?

She came back from Phoenix, and he held her tightly. He had missed her so.

They talked. Jim told her how, while she was away, he had done some hard thinking. "I've been a fool," he told her. "I realize how special you are, how special you are to me, and I want to try to make it work."

They talked more. He was once again the man she had fallen in love with. Days passed. Happy days, even though in the back of her mind the woman was cautious, trying to protect herself from disappointment.

It was at this time that she told him of her struggle to finish her book, and sensitive, knowing, he immediately understood her problem.

"You need to be honest with your readers," he said.

She nodded, telling him that she needed to share some part of her, some part of her life, her heart, that her readers needed this too.

"Do you trust in our relationship?" he asked her gently.

The woman looked at him a moment before she answered, knowing she must be truthful, then, "No," she answered.

As if he hadn't heard, Jim moved on. "Do you trust that I love you?" And this time, instantly, she answered that she did.

"Do you trust that you love me?" he asked her next. And with all her heart, and all the love in her heart, she replied that she did.

He took her hands in his, and looking into her eyes, he said lovingly, "You must write the truth, and whatever you write, whatever you say about me, and I know it could be bad, whatever it is, we will deal with it." Then, "I know you will write about my drinking. That's okay. It's the truth, and I would think less of you if you didn't write the truth."

"Do you realize that it could be unpleasant, that the whole world will know that you are an alcoholic?" she asked.

Jim nodded. "But it's okay," he said, "because we love each other, because ours is a very special love, and we will work it out."

She thought, "Oh, if only this were true, if only it could be this way."

And was she wrong to trust?

Two days passed. They were going out to dinner, and she was almost dressed and ready to go when Jim came home. It began almost as soon as he came through the door, and it was she who started it. Didn't she know better? Never argue with a man who's had a drink.

"Next time you're going to be late," she gently chided him, "would you mind calling and letting me know?"

His reaction was astonishing. He stormed and ranted, calling her a nag and worse, and as he stormed his face became redder and redder. His temper escalated until finally he stomped off down the stairs into the kitchen. The woman, shaken and upset, stood in the bathroom, gazing at her reflection in the mirror. She looked great. Her makeup was perfect. Her hair was just the way she liked it, the jacket she wore was a favorite. She was a perfect image. Successful, centered, well balanced. All the things she prided herself on. And who could see the scars, and who could see the pain . . . and who was looking anyway? Not Jim. Not Jim.

She drove him to the restaurant, not wanting him to drive himself, and on the way her life became a nightmare. He cursed and swore, and he was mean, so very mean to her, meaner than ever before.

The woman left him at the restaurant, knowing his friends would bring him home. For two days he ignored her; even when she tried to speak to him he would turn his back. He was so involved with himself, so self-righteous, so intent on blaming anyone and everything but himself, as had always been his way, that he did not see her needs, did not see that she was sick, saw nothing but his own misfortune.

She left, and was gone for a week. His first words to her when she came back were: "You left without a word. That wasn't a nice thing to do. And where were you? Where did you go?" They talked, and he was sorry, once again. "If I take another drink, I'll put a gun to my head and kill myself," he said.

And she looked on, compassion and love no longer clouding her thoughts, but her feelings toward him just as strong as ever. Then, quietly, gently, as he had his arms around her, she told him that she would no longer tolerate this kind of life. "I love you," she whispered to him softly, "and I would marry you tomorrow ... but I will stay with you only if your drinking stops."

For more than a week their life went well, and then the signs were there again. She would reach to kiss him, but he would screw up his mouth and turn his cheek to her. He would come home and instead of hugging her would place a kiss on her forehead. He smoked cigars, believing perhaps that they disguised the smell of alcohol. Of course they didn't.

"Maybe I'm wrong," she would think, knowing she was not. And he, when at last she mentioned it, denied emphatically that it was so.

She hadn't expected miracles, and if he lapsed it was okay, as long as he was trying. But how could she know when he refused to talk about it? How could she know? And all she could do now was love him.

> Oh the pain, and oh the suffering
> Humiliation, raw and bleeding
> All these lessons, meant to teach us
> All these trials, meant to mold us

And the pain? Not just hers, but his as well.

* * *

This chapter, this book, now drawing to its close, how will it end? I thumb through the pages I have just written, and these two paragraphs stand out among the rest:

And softly, and always softly, she heard his voice, as if carried on the wind.... "Trust, little one, trust."

She called again to God, not asking for a cure, not asking for a miracle, but asking now, "What can I learn from this? How can I grow from this? How strong can I become?"

I pause in my writing, thinking, thinking back, and again I reach into the manuscript. What am I looking for, what is it that I am striving toward? I am looking for strength, I am looking for courage, and I am desperately seeking inspiration.

I come upon the chapter "Rape."

It was time for the last dance.... Richard reached for me, and I knew I could not refuse.... I felt his arms tighten about me, felt his lips in my hair.... and then pictures flashed through my mind. I heard my ex-husband's voice... could hear his words, see the sneer on his face... "There is nothing," he said, "*nothing*, that I find attractive about you."

Another picture. I was almost fifteen... I had taken a cup of tea in to my mother... so fast, her hand shot out and grabbed my undershirt. She yanked it up, her face twisted with contempt as she looked at my still-undeveloped chest... I fled, shame and humiliation burning through me.

Another picture.... now I am small... I see myself, so small, so small, standing with bowed head. I hear my father's voice: "Lift up your hands, let me smell your fingers." I know he will smell me, I know he will beat me because I am so dirty... they tell me so... they tell me so... they must be right... they tell me so.

I feel his arms about me, so tender, so loving... Then the resolution—I will not be raped again—I will never accept rape passively again.

* * *

I think on this a moment, and recall the question I had asked Grey Eagle in Part 5, in the chapter "Questions." That question, so personal to me: "Grey Eagle, do you have any advice for those people striving to recover from alcohol or drug abuse?" I find the question, and in reading his answer, I come upon this:

"And so for each man or woman who takes a bottle and places it to his lips. . . . each man who does not take up the bottle is just as responsible."

How I understand Grey Eagle's words. How clearly I see that I must not be an enabler. That each time I turn a blind eye, or refuse to stand up and be counted, for whatever reason, I shirk my responsibility . . . to the world in which I live . . . to the universe and to God, whom I am a part of . . . to my fellow man and woman . . . and yes, last, but not least . . . to myself.

I read on: ". . . and when you find your behavior lacking in some way, and the outcome is confusion and anxiety . . . destruction . . . you will find that the root cause will be named fear. . . . fear of being still. . . . fear of recognizing one's own heart . . . fear of recognizing one's own soul. . . . fear, which stops the many from daring to look into that mirror . . ."

And on I read, and come then to this place . . . and as I read these words, I hear Grey Eagle's voice, clear, firm yet gentle . . . "And I will tell you, truly, and from my heart, they will only fail if there is a desire deep within them . . . buried deep, deep within them . . . they will only fail if that desire is to fail."

As I read, the words, the meaning of these words, touches my heart. I hear a truth, and I remember the seventh truth . . . "The truth is that which touches your heart, and echoes within the heart of your soul, which is God."

Again, once again, I thumb through the last pages now, and read, "I heard the heartbeat of my soul, I saw my broken heart, and then, with greater clarity than I had had before, I saw my love, my Jim." Then, farther back . . . "What can I learn from this? How can I grow from this? How strong can I become?"

What can I learn from this? How can I grow from this? Resolve grows strong within me. I feel it. I know it. I accept it.

The woman, now grown, now truly strong, and learning many lessons, more clearly sees her path. "I will never accept rape passively again."

She faces him, head on, her resolve strong. This is their only chance. "I want a commitment from you," she says, "a full and total commitment, to seek help, to work together, go for counseling, do whatever it takes together. The drinking has to stop."

At first he fights. She watches as he hides behind that wall he thinks protects him. Finally, he speaks: "This is my problem and I will do it alone."

Looking at him, her determination never weakening, she replies, "We do this together, work at this together, or I will leave."

He, equally determined, replies, "No."

It is only when she reaches her bedroom that the tears begin to flow. She cannot let him see her cry. He might presume she is still weak enough for him to win her over.

Three weeks pass. They talk again. They fight again. She cries again. Her resolve is just as strong. Now there are only three days left, before she leaves. This time she will not come back. This time she knows what she must do.

And how she hurts, and how she struggles, and yet her resolve grows stronger still.

"I must respect myself," she whispers. "I must live what I believe, must live all that I believe and teach, or I am nothing, and of no value to myself."

Only three days left. She has made it clear to him that she will not take one more step forward until he takes a step toward her. And even knowing all she knows, she does not know if he will take that step.

It is Wednesday morning. There is snow on the ground. She

is in bed, but awake. He is standing by the window looking out. He half-turns, runs his hands through his hair. "I don't know what to do," he says. "You have put me in a difficult position, and I don't know what to do."

She looks at him. She loves him, feels compassion for him in his confusion, but she has learned, and she is strong. "I did not put you in any position," she replies quietly, but firmly. "This is your choice. It is up to you."

His head bowed, shoulders slumped, he turns and looks fully at her. "Just tell me what to do, and I will do it," he says.

"I want your total commitment to resolving this problem. I want your promise that we will do this together as much as possible, that we will find someone to help us. And I want you to understand that I will hold you to this promise."

For one moment she thinks he will begin to argue again, then, nodding, he takes the first step. "Okay," he says, "I promise. We will do this together," and, turning, he leaves for work.

The woman lies still in her bed. Should she believe him? Was this just another promise? Only time will tell. But not too much time. For she knows, has learned, that she is too valuable a human being, too proud a spirit, to stay in a relationship where promises mean nothing.

As I write I hear a sound, a sound I have become familiar with, and one that I must heed. The sound grows louder, and comes from deep within, where all self-knowledge lies . . . and I become still, yet also writing, as I listen to the heartbeat of my soul. Its rhythm is strong, and becoming even stronger now, reminding me . . . that I am soul. That each human being, each creature on this earth, is light, and of the light.

And I look to my spirit, the light of my soul, and the heartbeat of my soul grows louder, reminds me again . . . that I am, simply, joyfully, now and forever, soul.

All that matters now is that I have in truth, in light, all that matters is that in truth, in light, I become more light, more truth.

Once more I hear Grey Eagle's voice, soft, gentle, as on the wind..."And we are spirit. And we are proud. All here who have risen from the mountain.

"And my name is Grey Eagle. And I am Apache. And I am spirit...and I am proud...Proud Spirit."

The heartbeat of my soul grows louder yet, the sound filling my ears. I hear myself call out, words come from deep within, within my heart...words which, though loud in my head, I whisper now...for now I know what I have learned. And I know how I can grow. And I know how strong I can become.

I speak those words, loud in my head, my voice strong and sure, yet the words spoken in whispered awe...and with Grey Eagle's hand upon my shoulder.

"And my name is Rosemary. And I am soul, and proud to be so. And I am spirit, even as I am human, with human faults and failings, even though I often fail, yet I try, and I am spirit, and am proud to be so. I am of God, and of the light, and of the universe, which is also of God, and yes, though tears fill my eyes, still I can see my light, and I am proud, proud that I am of God. With great humility, filled with compassion, full of love, and with God's good grace, I look to my soul...I hear its heartbeat. I look to my spirit, I recognize the warrior within, a gentle and a loving warrior, and, like Grey Eagle, and looking forward to the sun, I acknowledge that I too am proud...Proud Spirit.

EPILOGUE

Our attitude is everything. Is all. Tells us who we truly are. Dictates our todays and our tomorrows. Makes the difference in our lives. And only by looking back on yesterday, and on all the yesterdays which have gone before, only by looking back in total honesty, examining our actions, our motives, and the outcome of our actions, can we truly tell what our attitude has been, really understand if we need to change it.

It is so easy to become so involved with the day-to-day comings and goings in life. So easy to wear blinders, blame others, blame circumstances, for who we are, how we behave. The truth is we have nowhere else to look but to ourselves, and only when we are brave enough, desperate enough, to do this honestly can we ever change our lives for the better.

How can I help you, when I still struggle myself? How can I show you that you are spirit too? That you are soul, that you are of God? And who am I to suppose that you don't already know these things, that perhaps you are way ahead of me, that perhaps I should seek your help.

Are you proud to be soul?

Are you proud to be of God?

And are you proud to be spirit?

Then join with me, join hands with me, join light with me, join love with me. Unite with me, and let us all be proud... Proud Spirit.

TO CONTACT
ROSEMARY ALTEA

If you are interested in learning more about Rosemary Altea and her work, you can write to her at the following address:

Rosemary Altea
P.O. Box 25
Brigg
North Lincolnshire
South Humberside DN20 0SU
ENGLAND

If you wish to be placed on Rosemary's mailing list, please indicate that in your letter. Also, please let us know which of the following topics you are interested in learning more about:

- Private consultations
- Rosemary's healing tape, entitled *A Journey Toward Healing*
- Rosemary's healing organization, the RAAH
- Future books, audiotapes, and videotapes

Please make sure to clearly print your name, address, and fax number. Please enclose $3 to cover the cost of reply from overseas.

Rosemary is also the author of *The Eagle and the Rose*, available from Warner Books in hardcover, paperback, and on audiotape.

Give the Gift of Healing, a book and audiotape, will be available in October 1997 from Eagle Brook, an imprint of William Morrow.

For information about a signed, special limited edition of *Proud Spirit* ™, ask your local bookseller or write to:

Joann Davis
c/o Eagle Brook, an imprint of
William Morrow and Company, Inc.
1350 Avenue of the Americas
New York, N.Y. 10019